Sentence Combining and Paragraph Construction

Sentence Combining & Paragraph Construction

Katie Davis

The University of Southwestern Louisiana
Lafayette, Louisiana

MACMILLAN PUBLISHING CO., INC.
New York
COLLIER MACMILLAN PUBLISHERS
London

Copyright © 1983, Macmillan Publishing Co., Inc.
Printed in the United States of America

All rights reserved. No part of this book may be reproduced or
transmitted in any form or by any means, electronic or mechanical,
including photocopying, recording, or any information storage and
retrieval system, without permission in writing from the Publisher.

Macmillan Publishing Co., Inc.
866 Third Avenue, New York, New York 10022

Collier Macmillan Canada, Inc.

ISBN 0-02-327880-3

Library of Congress Cataloging in Publication Data

Davis, Katie Brittain Adams.
    Sentence combining and paragraph construction.

    Includes index.
    1. English language—Paragraphs.   2. English language
—Sentences.   I. Title.
PE1439.D38   808'.042   82-15291
ISBN 0-02-327880-3   AACR2

Printing: 1 2 3 4 5 6 7 8   Year: 3 4 5 6 7 8 9 0

ISBN   0-02-327880-3

To the memory of
Patricia Davis Martin

PREFACE

Sentence Combining and Paragraph Construction grew out of suggestions made by directors of English writing laboratories in universities and colleges located in eight different states. Personal contact with these directors as well as careful observation of their laboratory procedures made apparent the need for a supplementary text to be used by students with real difficulties in organizing logically developed sentences and paragraphs. The consensus of most laboratory directors interviewed was that students profit little from exercises in error recognition but that practice in writing, correcting, and rewriting has many more positive results.

Considerable research into various positive approaches to better writing has resulted in the conviction that practice in sentence combination is perhaps the most successful method of improving the writing of students enrolled in basic courses. This success obviously evolves from *two* facts: (1) Practice in writing sentences containing such structures as gerund, infinitive, and participial phrases as well as adjective and adverbial clauses makes the composition of sentences containing these structures intrinsic to the student; (2) the subject matter contained in the sentences to be combined expands the student's knowledge in such areas as geography and history and thus supplies him with the material necessary for writing sentences with substantial content.

The students using this text not only will learn the techniques of writing better sentences but will also be given practice in using this ability in writing good paragraphs developed according to the basic rhetorical modes. *Sentence Combining and Paragraph Construction* is not designed to be used as the only textbook for a basic writing course; rather, it is a supplementary text to be used along with a reader, such as *Comprehension and Composition* by Ann Dobie and Andrew Hirt, also published by Macmillan Publishing Company, Inc.

I am indebted to several people who have made the writing and publication of this book possible. They are Charlinda Davis Hebert, who provided the art work; Katherine D. Davis, who suggested the format; Edward Davis, Albert Fields, Ann Dobie, and Andrew Hirt, who provided the inspiration and constant encouragement; Sylvia Patterson and Kitty Simoneaux, who suggested that some of the exercises be used in the University of Southwestern Louisiana writing laboratory on an experimental basis; Sydney Lasseigne, who worked untiringly on the manuscript; and Tony English, the Macmillan editor, who patiently yet firmly insisted on the completion of the book. I am grateful to all of them.

Katie Davis

TO THE STUDENT!

Often during your college experience as well as during your career you will be called upon to write. Your success in writing will depend in large measure upon how well you have mastered the skills of writing good sentences and composing good paragraphs.

Of course, the very first step in the writing process is the construction of good sentences. Because this is true, the first twelve lessons of this book are designed to make you more aware of the various elements that make up a sentence, the ways these elements can be put together to form a good sentence, and the ways you can achieve sentence variety by using various combinations of these elements. Each of these twelve lessons contains valuable instructional material, such as definitions of sentence elements and appropriate examples of such elements, as well as adequate exercises designed to make the use of these elements an intrinsic part of your own writing. When you have completed the first twelve lessons, you will no doubt have mastered the technique of good sentence writing and will be better prepared to master the technique of good paragraph construction.

In Lessons 13 through 18 you will learn the art of good paragraph construction by learning how to write a thesis statement and how to use various methods in developing this thesis statement into a well-organized paragraph. These methods include example, definition, comparison and contrast, cause and effect, and classification and division. Numerous paragraphs developed by these methods are provided for your study. Most of these paragraphs are from one hundred to three hundred words in length. This does not mean that paragraphs cannot be shorter than one hundred words or longer than three hundred words. This length is used in the examples and also suggested for your writing because paragraphs of this length require careful development and are at the same time completely manageable.

When you have mastered the lessons on paragraph development, you will have solved many of the major problems of essay writing and will be well on your way to becoming a more competent writer.

Lessons 19 and 20 are included in order that you may be able to master some of the rules for correct spelling and punctuation, both of which are considered important in the writing process. The last lesson is one on grammar review. It is intended as a quick reference for those of you who need to have a particular grammatical term defined and illustrated.

Finally, the author has included an answer section that provides suggested solutions to the problems in the first exercise in each chapter. The solutions suggested in this section are by no means the only solutions. They are included to provide guidance for the student who is working toward his own solution.

The writing skills that you master as you proceed through the materials in this textbook will without doubt be reflected in the improved quality of your writing. In order to verify this improvement, at the end of the semester compare a paragraph you wrote early in the semester with one you wrote late in the semester. The improvement you note will perhaps surprise you but certainly will not fail to please you.

CONTENTS

Sentence Combining and Paragraph Construction

Basic Sentence Elements

ALL formal writing—whether it is personal, such as a letter; academic, such as an essay written in a history course; or professional, such as a report on monthly sales—begins with the sentence. It follows, then, that a thorough understanding of the basic elements of a sentence and of the ways these basic elements can be organized into a sentence is essential to good writing.

Our first question, then, is, "What is a sentence?" A sentence can be defined as a group of words containing a subject and a predicate that makes complete sense or expresses a complete thought. This definition, however, means almost nothing unless we know what a subject is and what a predicate is. The subject of a sentence is the word with all its modifiers that names the person, place, thing, or concept about which something is said. The predicate of a sentence is the word with all its modifiers that tells what the subject does or what the subject is. The subject and the predicate, then, are the basic elements of a sentence. Each of these two elements can consist of one word, as in

Dogs bark.

The word *dogs* is the subject because it names the thing about which something is said. The word *bark* is the predicate because it tells what the subject does. However, the subject as well as the predicate can consist of several words.

The two large, ferocious dogs in the back yard, which belong to my uncle, bark loudly at all strangers who come near them.

In this sentence the complete subject is *the two large, ferocious dogs in the back yard, which belong to my uncle.* The complete predicate is *bark at all strangers who come near them.* All the words in the subject except *dogs,* which is the simple subject, are modifiers; that is, they tell something about the dogs, their number, size, disposition, and owner. All the words in the complete predicate except the predicate verb *bark* are also modifiers; that is, they tell something about the frequency of the barking.

The modifiers of the subject as well as the modifiers of the predicate can be words, phrases, or clauses. In the preceding sentence, *two, large,* and *ferocious* are words that modify *dogs. In the back yard* is a phrase modifying *dogs,* and *which belong to my uncle* is a clause modifying *dogs.* By the same token, *loudly* is a word modifying *bark; at all strangers* is a phrase modifying *barks;* and *who come near them* is a clause modifying *strangers.*

A phrase can be defined as a group of words that functions as a unit but does not contain a subject and a predicate. When we say that a phrase functions as a unit, we mean that it functions as a noun or as a modifier. Phrases can be classified as prepositional phrases and as verbal phrases.

A prepositional phrase is one that is introduced by a preposition that is followed by a noun or a pronoun and its modifiers. Prepositions are words that are hard to define but easy to recognize. Frequently used prepositions include

in	before	at
on	behind	for
to	between	up
through	down	below
around	during	beneath
above	from	beside
under	into	along
about	off	inside
across	over	outside
after	underneath	against
among	toward	beyond

You will notice that most of these prepositions have something to do with position.

Prepositions followed by a noun and its modifiers are called prepositional phrases.

in the house	above the treetops
on the road	under the magnolia tree
for a purpose	about my grades
to the many students	across the green meadow
through the dark alley	after the lunch break
around the distant mountain	below the water

These prepositional phrases function as either adjectives or adverbs. When they function as adjectives, they tell something about places, persons, or things.

The house across the street is deserted.

The prepositional phrase *across the street* tells something about the thing *house* and is therefore a prepositional phrase functioning as an adjective.

The man in the red jacket is my father.

The prepositional phrase *in the red jacket* tells something about the word *man* and is therefore a prepositional phrase functioning as an adjective.

The furniture in the house is mine.

The prepositional phrase *in the house* tells something about the word *furniture*. It, too, is a prepositional phrase used as an adjective.

When the prepositional phrase tells something about a verb, that is, a word expressing action, being, or state of being; or when it tells something about an adjective, that is, a word that describes, numbers, or points out; or when it tells something about an adverb, that is, a word that says something about time, manner, or condition, the phrase is functioning as an adverb.

The soldiers marched down the road.

In this sentence the phrase *down the road* tells where the soldiers marched. Since it tells something about the action word *marched,* it is a prepositional phrase used as an adverb.

Phrases can also be classified as verbal phrases. A verbal phrase can be defined as a verb plus other words, all of which function as a noun or as a modifier. Verbal phrases can be classified as gerund phrases, as participial phrases, and as infinitive phrases. A gerund phrase is the *ing* form of the verb plus other words, all of which are used as a noun.

Mowing the grass is a tiresome job.

In this sentence *mowing the grass* is a gerund phrase made up of the *ing* verb *mowing* plus the other words *the grass,* all of which function as a noun, in this case as subject of the sentence.

A participial phrase is the *ing* or *ed* form of the verb used as a modifier of nouns.

The land occupied by the settlers was fertile.

In this sentence *occupied by the settlers* is a participial phrase made up of the *ed* form of the verb *occupy* plus other words, all of which tell something about the noun *land.*

Players entering this tennis tournament are the best in the nation.

In this sentence *entering this tennis tournament* is a participial phrase made up of the *ing* form of the verb *entering* plus other words, all of which tell something about the noun *players*.

An infinitive phrase is the word *to* plus a verb plus other words. An infinitive phrase can be used as a noun or as a modifier.

> To be a successful farmer was my father's lifelong ambition.

In this sentence the words *to be a successful farmer*, made up of the word *to* plus the verb *be* and other words, is an infinitive phrase used as a noun—in this case, as subject of the sentence.

> The way to achieve success is through hard work and determination.

In this sentence the words *to achieve success*, made up of *to* plus the verb *achieve* and another word *success*, is an infinitive phrase used as a modifier; that is, it identifies *the way*. A further explanation of verbal phrases can be found on pp. 81–83, 90–91, 99–100, and 203–205.

Phrases, whether prepositional or verbal, cannot function alone as sentences. They are, however, acceptable word groups that must be joined to other word groups to form sentences. For example, the word group

> in spite of his excellent grades

is not a complete sentence; it is a prepositional phrase. This word group, which, standing alone, does not express a complete thought, can be joined to other words to make the thought complete.

> In spite of his excellent grades, John was unhappy as a college student.

Another word group

> a successful businessman in our town

is made up of a prepositional phrase *in our town* plus the noun *businessman*, which the phrase modifies, and the other modifiers *a* and *successful*. Since the phrase does not express a complete thought, it is not a sentence. But when other words are added, it becomes a part of a complete sentence.

> A successful businessman in our town has established a scholarship for deserving students.

Let us look at still another word group:

> my father running for public office

This word group is made up of the participial phrase *running for public office* and the word it modifies, *father*, plus the pronoun *my*. Standing alone, it does not express a complete thought and is therefore not a sentence. By adding one word, the verb *is*, the word group becomes a complete sentence.

My father is running for public office.

The difference between a phrase and a clause is simply this: A phrase does not have a subject and a predicate; a clause does. When the clause forms a sentence, that is, when it expresses a complete thought or makes complete sense, it is called an independent clause. This means, essentially, that it can function alone, that it does not depend on additional words to make the thought expressed a complete thought. On the other hand, when the clause does not express a complete thought or make complete sense, it is called a dependent clause. This means that it cannot function or stand alone but that it depends on additional words in order to express a complete thought. The following clauses are independent. They have subjects and predicates and express complete thoughts.

Joan locked the doors and turned out the lights.
Chimpanzees live about forty years in their natural surroundings.
Balboa discovered the Pacific Ocean.
Louise Kincaid wants you to return the books immediately.
James Burns is our nominee.

The following groups of words are dependent clauses; they, too, have subjects and predicates, but they do not express complete thoughts:

after Joan locked the doors and turned off the lights
although chimpanzees live forty years in their natural surroundings
who discovered the Pacific Ocean
whose books you took by mistake
whom you are going to nominate

Each of these dependent clauses, when added to other word groups, can become complete sentences.

After Joan locked the doors and turned off the lights, she went to bed.
Although chimpanzees live forty years in their natural surroundings, they live only about half that time in captivity.
Vasco Nuñez de Balboa, who discovered the Pacific Ocean, was a Spaniard.
Louise Kincaid, whose books you took by mistake, wants you to return them immediately.
James Burns is the man whom you are going to nominate.

Sentences containing only one independent clause and no dependent clauses are called simple sentences. Simple sentences by all means should be used when you are writing letters, essays, and reports. However, to achieve sentence variety and thus improve your writing, you should not write a series of simple sentences but rather vary your sentence style by writing sentences containing two or more independent clauses, as well as those containing one or more dependent clauses.

EXERCISE 1
Basic Sentence Elements

In the following exercise add words to the phrases and clauses and thereby turn them into complete thoughts and thus into complete sentences. To illustrate, the word group

whenever you have completed your term paper

is a dependent clause. The thought is not complete. Additional information can turn the dependent clause into a complete sentence.

Whenever you have completed your term paper, you will have more time to concentrate on the examination review.

Furthermore, the word group

the Thames River, running through the city of London

contains a participial phrase *running through the city of London*, which modifies the noun *Thames River*. This word group does not express a complete thought until additional information is included.

The Thames River, running through the city of London, empties into the English Channel.

Again, the word group

that English composition is a required course

is a dependent clause and becomes a sentence only when more information is added.

All freshmen should know that English composition is a required course.

1. The city of London, which is the capital of Great Britain and Northern Ireland.

_____

_____

_____

2. The Westminster Bridge and the buildings where Parliament meets.

_____

_____

_____

3. St. Paul's Cathedral, a famous London landmark designed by Sir Christopher Wren.

_____

_____

_____

4. The British Museum, which is famous for its manuscripts, books, and art.

_____

_____

_____

5. Since London is located on the navigable Thames River.

_____

_____

_____

6. When London saw its population decline during the Great Plague of 1665.

_____

_____

_____

7. In 1666, as a result of the worst fire in London's history.

_____

_____

_____

8. When Germany bombed London during World War II.

_____

_____

_____

9. London, which is Great Britain's most important manufacturing and trading center.

_____

_____

_____

10. Although London is a large city.

_____

_____

_____

11. Because clay rather than granite lies under the surface of the city of London.

_____

_____

_____

12. Trafalgar Square, named for a great British naval victory.

_____

_____

_____

13. The Haymarket, lying to the west of Trafalgar Square.

_____

_____

_____

14. Plays written by playwrights from all over the world.

_____

_____

_____

15. Many bridges spanning the Thames River in the city of London.

_____

_____

_____

16. Tower Bridge to the east and London Bridge to the west.

_____

_____

_____

17. Westminster Bridge and Blackfriars Bridge, which are two other important and well-known bridges.

_____

_____

_____

18. Several parks, including Hyde Park and St. James Park.

_____

_____

_____

19. Regent's Park, containing the Zoological Gardens.

_____

_____

_____

20. The University of London, founded in 1836.

_____

_____

_____

After you have completed the exercise, refer to the section entitled "Suggested Answers" and examine two of several possible ways you can add words to the phrases and clauses and thereby turn them into complete thoughts and thus into complete sentences.

EXERCISE 2
Basic Sentence Elements

As in the previous exercise, add words to the phrases and clauses so that you express a complete thought and thus write a complete sentence.

1. Hawaii, which became the fiftieth state of the United States of America in 1959.

_____

_____

_____

2. The more than twenty beautiful tropical islands that make up the Hawaiian Islands.

_____

_____

_____

3. Hawaii Island, the largest of the islands and shaped like a triangle.

_____

_____

_____

4. Pearl Harbor, located on the island of Oahu.

_____

_____

_____

5. The red hibiscus, which is the official state flower.

_____

_____

_____

6. Polynesians from Tahiti.

_____

_____

_____

7. Captain James Cook, who discovered Hawaii in 1778.

_____

_____

_____

8. The islands that Captain Cook named the Sandwich Islands.

_____

_____

_____

9. After the first missionaries arrived in the islands.

_____

_____

_____

10. The natives living in Honolulu.

_____

_____

_____

11. Waikiki Beach, at one time a gathering place for Hawaiian kings and queens.

_____

_____

_____

12. Because Hawaii is the center of U.S. military activities in the Pacific Ocean.

_____

_____

_____

13. Sugar cane grown on seventy-five percent of the cultivated land.

_____

_____

_____

14. Pineapples, one of the most important crops in Hawaii.

_____

_____

_____

15. Since Hawaii has a mild climate, beautiful scenery, and clean, wide beaches.

_____

_____

_____

16. Luaus, featuring exotic food and hula dancing.

_____

_____

_____

17. *Aloha Oe*, which means *love to you.*

_____

_____

_____

18. Two musical instruments, the ukelele and the Hawaiian steel guitar.

_____

_____

_____

19. Although the first airplane flight to Hawaii from California in 1927 took twenty-seven hours.

_____

_____

_____

20. Today the thousands of tourists who fly to Hawaii every month.

_____

_____

_____

Compound Subjects

THIS exercise and the five that follow provide practice in combining simple sentences with no compound elements into longer, more complex structures in order to improve your writing. Although simple sentences with no compound elements should not be eliminated entirely from your writing, a variety of sentence structure adds quality to your composition. A simple sentence with no compound elements is one that contains only one independent clause, and this clause contains only one subject, one predicate verb, one direct object, one predicate nominative, or one predicate adjective.

It is important from the outset that we understand what these various sentence elements—subject, predicate verb, direct object, predicate nominative, predicate adjective—are. By definition, a subject is the word in the sentence about which something is said. Examine the following sentence.

George Washington was the first president of the United States.

In this sentence something is said about George Washington, specifically, that he was the first president of the United States. The subject of this sentence is therefore George Washington. Look at the next sentence.

Abraham Lincoln signed the Emancipation Proclamation in 1862.

In this sentence something is said about Abraham Lincoln, specifically, that he signed the Emancipation Proclamation. Therefore, Abraham Lincoln is the subject of the sentence. A further discussion of subjects can be found on p. 192. The subjects in the following sentences are italicized.

James A. Michener is a popular contemporary author.
Psychology is an interesting field of study.

Senators are not always in complete agreement with the president of the United States.

My *typewriter* is fifteen years old.

You know the penalties for breaking the speed limit.

The predicate verb in a sentence is the word in the sentence that tells what the subject did or what the subject is. If the verb tells what the subject did, it expresses action. If the predicate verb tells what the subject is, it expresses being or state of being. Look at the following sentences.

In 1776 the American colonies declared their independence from England.

In this sentence the word *declared* is an action verb telling what the colonists did. It is therefore the predicate verb of the sentence. Examine the next sentence.

John Adams was the first vice president of the United States.

The word *was* is the predicate verb of this sentence because it tells the state of being of John Adams. A further discussion of predicate verbs can be found on pp. 26–27 and 192. The predicate verbs in the following sentences are italicized.

Abraham Lincoln *decided* to become a lawyer.

He *succeeded* well in his chosen occupation.

He also *took* a keen interest in community affairs.

After several years, Lincoln *became* a member of Congress.

Finally, the American voters *elected* him president of the United States.

The direct object of a sentence is the word in the sentence that tells what receives the action of the verb. Therefore, a direct object must follow an action verb. Look at the following sentence.

Columbus discovered America.

The word *Columbus* is the subject of the sentence because something is said about Columbus; *discovered* is the predicate verb because it tells what action Columbus took. Now ask yourself the question, "What did Columbus discover?" The answer to that question, *America,* receives the action of the verb; that is, America was discovered. The word *America* is therefore the direct object. Now examine the next sentence.

F. Scott Fitzgerald wrote novels.

The word *wrote* is the action word or predicate verb. Ask yourself the question, "What was written?" The answer to that question, *novels,* tells what receives the action of the verb and is therefore the direct object. A further discussion of direct objects can be found on pp. 37–40 and 192. The direct objects in the following sentences are italicized.

> Ulysses S. Grant led the Union *forces* during the War Between the States.
> As a young man, Grant liked *horses.*
> Soon after he became commander of the Union forces, Grant captured *Fort Henry.*
> He then defeated the *Confederates* at Shiloh.
> General Grant won the *confidence* of the president.

A predicate nominative is the word in the sentence that follows the predicate verb and renames the subject of the sentence. A predicate verb cannot follow an action verb but must follow a verb that expresses being or state of being. Study the following sentence.

> Ann Dobie is chairman of freshman English.

In this sentence the words *chairman* and *Ann Dobie* are one and the same; that is, the word *chairman* renames the subject *Ann Dobie.* You will note that the words can be reversed without changing the meaning of the sentence.

> The chairman of freshman English is Ann Dobie.

In the first of these two sentences, the word *chairman* comes after the predicate verb and renames the subject *Ann Dobie.* The word *chairman* is therefore the predicate nominative. In the second sentence the words *Ann Dobie* follow the predicate verb and rename the subject. *Ann Dobie* is therefore the predicate nominative. Examine the next sentence.

> Pat Morgan is my English instructor.

The word *instructor,* since it comes after the predicate verb and renames the subject *Pat Morgan,* is the predicate nominative. The order of the two nouns can be reversed.

> My English instructor is Pat Morgan.

In this sentence the words *Pat Morgan* come after the predicate verb and rename the subject *my English instructor.* The predicate nominative is therefore *Pat Morgan.* (A further discussion of predicate nominatives can be found on pp. 49–52 and 194.) The predicate nominatives in the following sentences are italicized.

> During the War Between the States, Robert E. Lee was the *commander* of the Confederate Army.
> Robert E. Lee's father was a Revolutionary War *general.*
> Lee's most effective helper was *General Stonewall Jackson.*
> Another of Lee's helpers was *Jeb Stuart.*

The defeat at Gettysburg was a crushing *blow* to the hopes of the South.

Finally, a predicate adjective is a word that follows the predicate verb and describes or limits the subject of the sentence. A predicate adjective, like a predicate nominative, never follows an action verb but rather follows a verb that expresses being or state of being. Examine the following sentence.

The ducks in the pond are too numerous to count.

The word *numerous* comes after the predicate verb *are* and tells how many ducks were in the pond. The word *numerous* is therefore a predicate adjective because it limits the number of ducks in the pond. Look at the next sentence.

My favorite crackers are crisp and salty.

The words *crisp* and *salty* describe the subject of the sentence *crackers;* that is, the two words tell what kind of crackers are my favorite. Since the words *crisp* and *salty* come after the predicate verb *are* and describe the subject *crackers,* these two words are predicate adjectives. A further discussion of predicate adjectives can be found on pp. 193–194. The predicate adjectives in the following sentences are italicized.

General Sheridan was *kind* and *friendly* toward his soldiers.
In battle he was *courageous, devoted,* and *skillful.*
In manner General Grant was *quiet* and *dignified.*
General Lee was *simple-hearted* and *frank.*
After the war was over, General Grant and General Lee remained *popular* with their countrymen.

Many times you will find that two or more sentences can be combined by using two or more subjects, predicate verbs, direct objects, predicate nominatives, or predicate adjectives in a single sentence. In this text the six lessons on compound elements provide practice in the use of compound elements as a means of tightening your sentence structure by eliminating superfluous or unnecessary words. The first of these six lessons is designed to help you learn to use compound subjects as a means of improving your sentence structure. For example, the three sentences

Rice is an important crop grown in south Louisiana.
Sugar cane is another important crop grown in south Louisiana.
For some south Louisiana farmers, soybean cultivation is important.

can be combined by writing one sentence containing a compound subject.

Rice, sugar cane, and soybeans are three important crops grown in south Louisiana.

Sometimes two or more sentences can be combined by using a compound subject and rephrasing the rest of the information supplied in the sentences. To illustrate, the three sentences

The Pinto is a small economy car that averages about thirty-two miles per gallon of gasoline.
The Honda is a small car that gets about thirty-five miles to a gallon of gasoline.
The Vega, another small car, runs about twenty-nine miles on one gallon of gasoline.

can be combined by using a compound subject and rephrasing the information supplied in the rest of the sentences. One possibility is:

The Pinto, the Honda, and the Vega are small economy cars that average between twenty-nine and thirty-five miles per gallon of gasoline.

Occasionally, in order to use a compound subject as a means of eliminating unnecessary words and thus tightening your sentence structure, you may have to change a predicate nominative to a subject. For example, in the second of the following three sentences:

Landscape painting was one of Winston Churchill's favorite hobbies.
Winston Churchill was an amateur bricklayer.
Trout fishing gave Winston Churchill many hours of enjoyable leisure.

the predicate nominative *amateur bricklayer* will have to be changed to a subject *amateur bricklaying* in order to make this leisure-time activity one of the three subjects of the sentence along with landscape painting and trout fishing. The three sentences can then be combined into one sentence containing a compound subject.

Landscape painting, amateur bricklaying, and trout fishing were Winston Churchill's favorite leisure-time activities.

EXERCISE 1
Compound Subjects

In this exercise you are to combine the sentences in each group by writing one sentence that contains a compound subject. Again, when you have completed the exercise, refer to the section entitled "Suggested Answers" and examine some of the possible ways the sentences can be combined.

1. Australia is an island country in the South Pacific.
2. New Zealand is also an island country located in the South Pacific.

Group 1

_____

_____

1. North Island is one of the three large islands that make up the country of New Zealand.
2. South Island is another of the large New Zealand islands.
3. The third large island in New Zealand is Steward Island.

Group 2

_____

_____

_____

1. Wellington, the capital of New Zealand and one of its largest cities, is located on North Island.
2. Another large city located on North Island is Auckland, the chief New Zealand port.

Group 3

_____

_____

1. One of the chief sources of farm income in New Zealand is dairy farming.
2. Sheep raising is one of two main sources of farm income in New Zealand.

Group 4

_____

_____

1. Most New Zealanders speak English.
2. Maori is another language spoken in New Zealand.

Group 5

_____

_____

1. Sydney, the capital of New South Wales, is one of Australia's largest cities.
2. Melbourne, the capital of Victoria, is the second largest city in Australia.
3. The third largest city in Australia is Brisbane, the capital of Queensland.

Group 6

_____

_____

_____

1. William Dampier was the first English explorer to visit Australia.

Group 7

2. James Cook, an English sea captain, was the second Englishman to visit Australia.

_____

_____

Group 8
1. Willem Jansz, a Dutchman, was the first European to visit Australia.
2. Another Dutchman, Abel Tasman, was the second European to report the existence of Australia.

_____

_____

Group 9
1. The duckbilled platypus is one of Australia's strangest animals.
2. Another strange animal that can be found in Australia is the emu.
3. Australia is one of three continents where the lungfish, an unusual but highly developed fish, can be found.

_____

_____

_____

Group 10
1. The wombat, a marsupial, or an animal that when young is carried in an outside pouch on its mother, lives in Australia.
2. Another Australian marsupial is the kangaroo.
3. Koalas are also marsupials that live in Australia.

_____

_____

_____

Group 11
1. The eucalyptus tree, which is native to Australia, is the most frequently seen tree on the continent.
2. Another popular Australian tree is the wattle, or acacia, which grows in the dry inland regions.

_____

_____

Group 12
1. Sugar cane is the leading crop grown along the tropical northeastern coast of Australia.
2. Pineapples, which require much warmth and moisture, also grow well in Australia's northeastern coastal area.

_____

_____

Group 13
1. Cool summers along the southeastern coastal plains of Australia are good for dairy farming.
2. Abundant rainfall, which makes the grass grow well, also en-

courages dairy farming along the southeastern Australian coastal plains.

3. An important market for dairy products can be found in the large Australian cities lying along the southeastern coast.

_____

_____

_____

1. West of the Eastern Highlands, which divide the coastal plains from the rest of Australia, sheep rather than dairy cattle are raised.
2. In the plains west of the Eastern Highlands, wheat is the principal crop.

Group 14

_____

_____

1. Wheat is one of the two principal Australian exports.
2. Australia exports more wool than any other country in the world.

Group 15

_____

_____

1. Dingoes, or wild Australian dogs, are a constant danger to sheep.
2. Rabbits, brought to Australia by early settlers, eat vast quantities of grass in sheep-growing country.
3. Frequently droughts dry up the pasture lands and sheep can not get enough food.

Group 16

_____

_____

_____

1. Manufacturing is the largest source of income in Australia.
2. Mining is also important in the Australian economy.
3. Trade with other countries contributes to the economic well-being of Australia.

Group 17

_____

_____

_____

1. One of Australia's principal export markets is the British Commonwealth of Nations.
2. Japan buys great quantities of Australian wool.
3. Australian beef is exported to the United States.

Group 18

_____

_____

_____

Group 19

1. Australia is a leading world producer of lead.
2. Gold is found in large quantities in Australia.
3. There are many silver and zinc mines in Australia.

_____

_____

_____

Group 20

1. In 1949 uranium deposits were discovered in northern Australia.
2. Oil was discovered in western Australia in 1953.

_____

_____

When you have completed this exercise, write five original sentences containing compound subjects.

1. _____

_____

_____

2. _____

_____

_____

3. _____

_____

_____

4. _____

_____

_____

5. _____

_____

_____

EXERCISE 2
Compound Subjects

As in the previous exercise, combine the sentences in each group by writing one sentence that contains a compound subject.

Group 1

1. Nevada has many popular ski resorts.
2. Utah attracts many skiing enthusiasts from all over the United States.
3. Colorado's resorts are popular during the skiing season.

_____

_____

_____

1. Fisherman's Wharf is a popular tourist attraction in San Francisco.
2. Picturesque cable cars are one of San Francisco's main tourist attractions.
3. Most tourists in San Francisco visit the Golden Gate Bridge and the Golden Gate Bridge Park.

Group 2

_____

_____

_____

1. Tourists from all over the world visit New Orleans each year for the pre-Lenten celebration called Mardi Gras.
2. The Vieux Carré or French Quarter is the most famous year-round tourist attraction in New Orleans.
3. St. Louis Cathedral and the Cabildo are two buildings that visitors to New Orleans want to see.

Group 3

_____

_____

_____

1. One of the most famous and elegant restaurants in New Orleans is Antoine's.
2. Broussard's in New Orleans' French Quarter is famous for its French cuisine.
3. Le Ruth's is considered to be one of the finest restaurants in New Orleans.

Group 4

_____

_____

_____

1. St. Patrick's Cathedral on Fifth Avenue welcomes hundreds of New York City visitors each day.
2. A trip to New York City would be incomplete without a visit to the Statue of Liberty.
3. The United Nations buildings attract many tourists to New York.

Group 5

_____

_____

_____

1. The Metropolitan Museum of Art in New York City has one of the finest collections of traditional paintings and sculpture in the United States.
2. The Museum of Modern Art in New York City houses contemporary paintings and sculpture.

Group 6

3. The Guggenheim Museum in New York City is famous for its unusual architectural design.

_____
_____
_____

Group 7

1. The greatest railroad center in the United States is located in Chicago, Illinois.
2. Chicago is one of the largest meat-packing centers in the United States.
3. Chicago is famous for its steel production.

_____
_____
_____

Group 8

1. The Columbian Exposition, celebrating the four-hundredth anniversary of the discovery of America, was held in Chicago in 1893.
2. A Century of Progress, celebrating the hundredth anniversary of the founding of the city, was held in 1933.

_____
_____

Group 9

1. Faneuil Hall, or the Cradle of American Liberty, is toured annually by the many visitors to Boston, Massachusetts.
2. The Old South Meeting Hall, where the Boston Tea Party began, attracts tourists to Boston.
3. The Old North Church, from which Paul Revere received his signals, is one of Boston's leading tourist attractions.

_____
_____
_____

Group 10

1. The Lincoln Memorial is visited annually by thousands of tourists in Washington, D.C.
2. Many tourists feel that a visit to Washington, D.C., would be incomplete without a visit to the Washington Monument.
3. The Jefferson Memorial is a popular tourist attraction in Washington, D.C.

_____
_____
_____

Group 11

1. The Museum of Natural History is one of the most popular buildings in Washington's Smithsonian Institution.

2. The Smithsonian Institution also includes the popular National Air Museum.
3. The National Gallery of Art, a part of Washington's Smithsonian Institution, is popular with visitors to Washington, D.C.

_____

_____

_____

1. A trip to Washington, D.C., would be incomplete without a visit to the White House, the home of the president of the United States.
2. A visit to the Archives Building, which houses the most valuable documents of the United States, should be part of any trip to Washington, D.C.
3. The United States Capitol, which contains the chambers of the House of Representatives and the Senate, is visited daily by hundreds of tourists in Washington, D.C.

Group 12

_____

_____

_____

1. The Declaration of Independence can be seen in the Archives Building in Washington, D.C.
2. The Archives Building houses the Constitution of the United States.

Group 13

_____

_____

1. Colorado's Rocky Mountain National Park is the nation's favorite camping ground.
2. Many camping enthusiasts visit Colorado's Mesa Verde National Park every year.

Group 14

_____

_____

1. Among the most popular resort centers of Florida are Palm Beach and Miami on the Atlantic coast.
2. St. Petersburg and Tampa on the Gulf of Mexico are famous Florida resort cities.

Group 15

_____

_____

1. Mammoth Cave in Kentucky is one of the world's most famous caverns.

Group 16

2. Carlsbad Caverns in New Mexico are world-famous under-ground caves.

_____

_____

Group 17

1. One of Tennessee's many tourist attractions is the Hermitage, home of Andrew Jackson.
2. Many tourists visit the Great Smoky Mountains National Park in Tennessee.
3. An exact copy of the Greek Parthenon can be seen in Nashville, Tennessee.

_____

_____

_____

Group 18

1. La Villita, or Spanish Village, is located in the heart of San Antonio, Texas.
2. Another of San Antonio's landmarks, the Alamo, is located near La Villita.
3. The Hemisfair Tower is located in downtown San Antonio.

_____

_____

_____

Group 19

1. The Aerospace Medical Center at Brooks Air Force Base is an important military installation located in San Antonio, Texas.
2. Fort Sam Houston, the Fourth United States Army headquarters, is also located in San Antonio.
3. Four United States Air Force bases, Brooks, Lackland, Kelly, and Randolph, can be found in San Antonio.

_____

_____

_____

Group 20

1. St. Philip's Church in Charleston, South Carolina, is a historic Southern landmark.
2. The Citadel, a famous military college, is located in Charleston.
3. Fort Sumter, where the first shots of the Civil War were fired, is a Charleston monument.

_____

_____

_____

After you have completed the exercise, write five original sentences containing compound subjects.

1. _____

_____

_____

2. _____

_____

_____

3. _____

_____

_____

4. _____

_____

_____

5. _____

_____

_____

Compound Predicate Verbs

THIS exercise provides practice in combining simple sentences containing no compound elements into longer, more complex structures in order to improve your writing. Although simple sentences should be used at times to provide sentence variety, a good writer adds quality to his compositions by alternating simple sentences with other more complicated structures. In this lesson practice is provided in the use of compound predicates as a means of gaining variety of sentence structure as well as a means of tightening your sentence structure. Let us review the definition of predicates in order that you may more easily identify this particular sentence element. As you probably remember, the complete subject of a sentence is the word, plus all its modifiers, that names the person, place, thing, or concept about which something is said in the sentence. The complete predicate of a sentence is the word, plus all its modifiers, that tells what the subject does or what the subject is. Remember, too, that modifiers are words that answer such questions as "How many?" "What kind?" "Which one?" "How?" "When?" "Where?" "For what reason?" In the following sentences the complete predicates are italicized.

The migration of the whites to the far West *alarmed the Indians.*
The Indians *complained about the slaughter of wild animals.*
The whites *made treaties with the Indians.*
However, treaties *were broken* and war *ensued.*
Many Indians and whites *were slaughtered during these wars.*

Many times you will find that two or more sentences with the same subject can be combined into one sentence if you will give this sentence a compound predicate. For example, the three sentences that follow—

William Shakespeare wrote plays.
William Shakespeare produced plays.
William Shakespeare was also a director.

can be combined by writing a sentence that contains a compound predicate verb:

William Shakespeare wrote, produced, and directed plays.

By such combination not only will you eliminate unnecessary words and thus tighten your sentence structure but you will also achieve sentence variety and thus improve your style. Look at the next three sentences.

George Sebastian carefully fastened his helmet.
He then jumped astride his motorcycle.
Then he raced down the street at a dangerously high speed.

These sentences can be combined by writing a sentence that contains a compound predicate verb:

George Sebastian carefully fastened his helmet, jumped astride his motorcycle, and raced down the street at a dangerously high speed.

Sometimes the order of the words in a sentence or clause will have to be changed when combining predicates in order to achieve a balanced structure in the compound predicate. For example, the three sentences

My cousin George hunts deer in Texas during the Thanksgiving holidays.
During Christmas vacation George skis in Colorado.
George spends his Easter break surfing in Hawaii.

require some change in word order before you can combine them into one sentence containing a compound predicate.

My cousin George hunts deer in Texas during the Thanksgiving holidays, skis in Colorado during the Christmas vacation, and surfs in Hawaii during the Easter break.

EXERCISE 1
Compound Predicate Verbs

In the following exercise you are to combine the sentences in each group by writing one sentence that contains a compound predicate verb or a compound complete predicate. Again, when you have completed the exercise, refer to the section entitled "Suggested Answers" and examine one of the possible ways each sentence can be rephrased.

Group 1
1. The cowboy mounted his dapple-gray horse.
2. He then picked up the reins.
3. Then he went off in search of the stray cow.

_____

_____

_____

Group 2
1. Dr. Hirt walked to the lectern.
2. He opened his notebook.
3. Then he began his lecture on Greek drama.

_____

_____

_____

Group 3
1. Mrs. Dobie started her car.
2. She backed down the driveway.
3. Then she hit a tree.

_____

_____

_____

Group 4
1. The comedian walked to the edge of the stage.
2. He looked at the audience.
3. He then began to tell outrageously funny stories.

_____

_____

_____

Group 5
1. Indians in Santa Fe, New Mexico, make jewelry.
2. They sell jewelry they make to tourists visiting Santa Fe.

_____

_____

Group 6
1. Benjamin Franklin, one of America's great statesmen, invented bifocal glasses.
2. Benjamin Franklin also discovered that lightning is a huge spark of electricity.
3. Benjamin Franklin started the magazine that became the _Saturday Evening Post_.

_____

_____

_____

Group 7
1. Galagos, or "bush babies," which are strange little animals found in Africa, hunt for their food at night.
2. During the daytime, the galago curls itself up in a tree.

3. The galago sleeps until dusk.

_____

_____

_____

1. The Federal Bureau of Investigation solves crimes committed against the United States.
2. The FBI also investigates the backgrounds of government workers.
3. The FBI guards against enemy spies during wartime.

_____

_____

_____

Group 8

1. James Madison helped write the Constitution of the United States.
2. Under Thomas Jefferson, James Madison served as Secretary of State.
3. James Madison became the fourth president of the United States.

_____

_____

_____

Group 9

1. Farmers in Spain cultivate grapes to be distilled into wine.
2. Spanish farmers grow olives to be processed into oil.
3. Farmers in Spain raise tobacco to be made into cigarettes and cigars.

_____

_____

_____

Group 10

1. The sandpiper lives on the seashore.
2. Sandpipers dig in the sand for insects.
3. Sandpipers follow receding waves searching for shellfish.

_____

_____

_____

Group 11

1. Daniel Boone, a famous American pioneer, fought against the Indians.
2. Boone helped to settle the state of Kentucky.
3. Finally, Boone moved his family to Missouri.

_____

_____

_____

Group 12

Group 13   1. During World War I, Douglas MacArthur, a graduate of the United States Military Academy at West Point, fought with the Allied forces in France.
2. Douglas MacArthur was supreme commander of the Allied forces in the South Pacific during World War II.
3. During the Korean conflict, MacArthur served as overall commander of the United Nations forces.

Group 14   1. Herbert Hoover served as head of the American Relief Administration in Europe after World War I.
2. Under both President Harding and President Coolidge, Hoover was Secretary of Commerce.
3. Herbert Hoover became the thirty-first president of the United States.

Group 15   1. Susan B. Anthony, a pioneer in the fight for women's rights, advocated the abolition of slavery.
2. The first state temperance society was founded by Susan B. Anthony.
3. Susan B. Anthony was largely responsible for the passage of the 19th Amendment, which gave women the right to vote.

Group 16   1. Chester Nimitz served in the submarine fleet during World War I.
2. During World War II Nimitz was Allied commander of the Pacific Fleet.
3. After World War II Nimitz became a cabinet advisor to the Secretary of the Navy.

Group 17   1. William Penn, a pioneer American, founded the state of Pennsylvania.
2. Penn planned the city of Philadelphia.
3. William Penn helped in uniting the American colonies in their revolt against England.

---

1. William Howard Taft was named Secretary of War in Theodore Roosevelt's cabinet.
2. Taft was elected the twenty-seventh president of the United States in 1908.
3. In 1921 Taft was appointed chief justice of the United States Supreme Court.

_____
_____
_____

1. Voltaire, one of the most important French writers and thinkers, composed satirical verse.
2. Voltaire wrote a short novel, *Candide.*
3. Voltaire attacked the church and the state in his *Philosophic Dictionary*, a collection of essays on a wide variety of subjects.

_____
_____
_____

1. Robert Edwin Peary, a famous explorer, discovered the North Pole in 1909.
2. Peary proved that the North Pole was the center of a large, ice-covered sea.
3. Peary also claimed that Greenland was an island.

_____
_____
_____

After you have completed this exercise, write five original sentences containing compound predicate verbs or compound complete predicates.

1. _____
_____
_____
2. _____
_____
_____
3. _____
_____
_____
4. _____
_____
_____
5. _____

EXERCISE 2
Compound Predicate Verbs

Again you are to combine each of the following groups of sentences into one sentence by using a compound predicate verb or a compound complete predicate.

Group 1

1. Henry the Navigator, a fifteenth-century Portuguese seaman, explored several islands off the coast of Africa.
2. Henry later founded a school for navigators.

Group 2

1. Christopher Columbus believed in the theory that the earth was round.
2. He organized an expedition to reach Asia by sailing westward.
3. On this voyage he discovered America.

Group 3

1. Vasco da Gama, a Portuguese navigator, was asked by his king to make a sea voyage to India.
2. He sailed from Lisbon with four ships.
3. Da Gama became the first man to reach India by sailing around the southern tip of Africa.

Group 4

1. Vasco Nuñez de Balboa, a Spanish explorer, sailed to America in 1500.
2. He discovered the Pacific Ocean in 1513 and claimed it for Spain.

Group 5

1. Hernando Cortez, sailing under the flag of Spain, reached Mexico in 1519.
2. By 1521 he had completed the conquest of Mexico.
3. In 1536 he discovered Lower or Baja California.

1. Hernando de Soto explored and conquered Florida for Spain in 1539.
2. He then pushed westward in search of gold.
3. De Soto discovered the Mississippi River in 1541.

Group 6

_____

_____

_____

1. Jacques Cartier, a French explorer, made three voyages to Canada in the sixteenth century.
2. He discovered and explored the St. Lawrence River in 1534–1535.
3. Cartier claimed vast areas of land along the St. Lawrence River for France.

Group 7

_____

_____

_____

1. Francisco Coronado, a Spanish explorer, went up the Colorado River and discovered the Grand Canyon in 1540.
2. Coronado explored the area now known as the Texas Panhandle and Oklahoma.
3. He claimed much of the southwestern part of the United States for Spain.

Group 8

_____

_____

_____

1. Sir Francis Drake, noted for his role in the defeat of the Spanish Armada in 1588, made three expeditions to the West Indies.
2. He crossed the Isthmus of Panama and thus became the first Englishman to see the Pacific Ocean.
3. In 1580 he became the first Englishman to sail around the globe.

Group 9

_____

_____

_____

1. Sir Walter Raleigh, English navigator, historian, poet, and favorite of Queen Elizabeth, made several unsuccessful attempts to colonize Virginia.
2. He did, however, introduce potatoes and tobacco into England.

Group 10

3. Many years later he searched for gold along the Orinoco River in Venezuela.

_____

_____

_____

Group 11
1. Samuel de Champlain, sailing under the flag of France, explored the northeastern part of the North American coast.
2. Champlain discovered the beautiful lake that bears his name.
3. In 1608, with a group of settlers, Champlain founded Quebec.

_____

_____

_____

Group 12
1. Henry Hudson, a seventeenth-century English navigator, attempted to discover a northeast passage to India.
2. He discovered the Hudson River in 1609.
3. In 1611 he reached Hudson Bay.

_____

_____

_____

Group 13
1. Abel Tasman, a Dutch mariner, explored the waters around Australia.
2. In 1642 he discovered Tasmania, which he named Van Dieman's Land.
3. On his second voyage in 1644, he discovered the Gulf of Carpentaria.

_____

_____

_____

Group 14
1. Jacques Marquette, a French Jesuit missionary, explored the Great Lakes area of North America.
2. He founded the mission of St. Ignace on the north shore of the Straits of Mackinac in 1671.
3. With Louis Jolliet, Marquette explored the Wisconsin and Mississippi Rivers to the mouth of the Arkansas River.

_____

_____

_____

Group 15
1. Robert Cavelier, Sieur de La Salle, a French explorer and settler, descended the Mississippi River to the Gulf of Mexico in 1682.

2. He claimed the entire Mississippi Valley for France.

3. In honor of Louis XIV, he named the area Louisiana.

_____

_____

_____

1. Vitus Bering, a Danish explorer in the service of Russia, attempted to determine whether Asia and North America were connected.

2. In 1728 he discovered the sea and the straits which now bear his name and which separate the two continents.

_____

_____

Group 16

1. James Cook, an eighteenth-century English explorer, made two unsuccessful attempts to find a large continent in the South Pacific.

2. In 1776 he headed an unsuccessful attempt to find a northern route to India.

3. He discovered the Hawaiian Islands in 1778.

_____

_____

_____

Group 17

1. Together Meriweather Lewis and William Clark led an expedition to explore the Louisiana Purchase.

2. Lewis and Clark went up the Missouri River to its source.

3. They crossed the Great Divide and descended the Columbia River to the Pacific Ocean.

_____

_____

_____

Group 18

1. Roald Amundsen, a Norwegian polar explorer, successfully located the North Magnetic Pole.

2. He sailed through the Northwest Passage into Beaufort Sea and on through Bering Strait.

3. In 1911 he discovered the South Pole.

_____

_____

_____

Group 19

1. Richard Byrd, a United States aviator, explorer, and naval officer, flew over the North Pole in 1926 and the South Pole in 1929.

Group 20

2. Byrd made five exploratory expeditions to the Antarctic between 1928 and 1955.
3. During World War II Byrd served with the United States fleet both in Washington and overseas.

_____

_____

_____

_____

When you have completed this exercise, write five original sentences containing a compound predicate verb or a compound complete predicate.

1. _____

_____

_____

2. _____

_____

_____

3. _____

_____

_____

4. _____

_____

_____

5. _____

_____

_____

Compound Direct Objects

THIS exercise provides practice in combining direct objects in order to tighten your sentence structure by eliminating unnecessary words and thus write more effectively. First let us define the term *direct object*. Words, phrases, and clauses can be used as direct objects. These words, phrases, or clauses follow the predicate verb and receive the action of that verb. In sentences that contain a direct object, the verb must be an action verb, such as *sing, write, make, bring, take, seek,* and hundreds more. If you ask yourself,

> What was sung?
> What was written?
> What was made?
> What was brought?
> What was sought?

the answer to the question serves as a clue to the identification of the direct object.

For example, in the sentence

> The choir sang Handel's *Messiah*.

the action word is *sang*. Ask yourself the question "What was sung?" The answer is, of course, Handel's *Messiah*, which is the direct object.

Furthermore, in the sentence

> John Milton wrote *Paradise Lost*.

Paradise Lost (which answers the question "What was written?") is the direct object of the verb *wrote*.

Again, in the sentence

> Japanese auto workers make the Toyota.

Toyota answers the question "What is made?" and is therefore the direct object of the verb *make*.

Sometimes the direct object can be a gerund or a gerund phrase. A gerund can be defined as a verb used as a noun. This verb has the *ing* ending. For example, when the words *skiing*, *surfing*, and *hunting* are used as nouns, as in

Skiing is my favorite winter sport.
My cousin enjoys surfing.
Jeffrey dislikes hunting.

they are called gerunds. In the first sentence *skiing* is a gerund used as the subject of the sentence. In the second sentence *surfing* is a gerund used as a direct object answering the question "What was enjoyed?" In the third sentence *hunting* is a gerund used as a direct object answering the question "What did Jeffrey dislike?" In the following sentences the gerunds are italicized.

Reading is my favorite indoor activity. (*Reading* is the subject of the sentence.)
Bowling is a sport that requires good body coordination. (*Bowling* is the subject of the sentence.)
My father dislikes *traveling*. (*Traveling* is the direct object answering the question "What does my father dislike?")
Gourmets enjoy *eating* and *drinking*. (*Eating* and *drinking* are direct objects answering the question "What do gourmets enjoy?")
Hunting is my brother's favorite sport. (*Hunting* is the subject of the sentence.)

A gerund phrase is an *ing* verb, with its modifiers and objects, that is used as a noun. For example, in the sentence

After the accident Jonathan stopped driving his car recklessly.

the words *driving his car recklessly* constitute a gerund phrase containing the gerund *driving*, the direct object of the gerund *his car*, and the adverbial modifier *recklessly*. A close examination of this sentence will reveal that although a gerund is used as a noun, it has the properties of a verb—in this case a direct object and an adverbial modifier. In the following sentences the gerund phrases are italicized.

Drilling for oil in the Gulf of Mexico requires enormous expenditures of money. (Subject of the sentence.)
Balancing the federal budget seems to be an impossible task. (Subject of the sentence.)
My cousin John enjoys *fishing for trout in Vermilion Bay*. (Direct object answering the question "What does my cousin John enjoy?")
The referee penalized the team for *delaying the game*. (Object of the preposition *for*.)
After the Christmas holidays, I will consider *going on a diet*. (Direct object answering the question "What will I consider?")

Infinitives and infinitive phrases can also be used as direct objects. An infinitive is the word *to* plus a verb. For example, *to fish, to sleep, to drive* are infinitives and can be used as direct objects. The sentence

Joshua vacationed in Florida because he wanted to fish.

contains the infinitive *to fish*, which answers the question "What did Joshua want?" and is therefore the direct object of the verb *wanted*. Likewise, in the sentence

After being up all night, Mary Jane needed to sleep.

the infinitive *to sleep* is the direct object because it answers the question "What did Mary Jane need?" The infinitives in the following sentences are italicized.

The captain refused *to surrender.* (Direct object answering the question "What did the captain refuse to do?")
You failed the test because you refused *to study.* (Direct object answering the question "What did you refuse to do?")
I want *to succeed.* (Direct object answering the question "What do I want?")
Mary decided *to resign.* (Direct object answering the question "What did Mary decide?")
He asked *to be excused.* (Direct object answering the question "What did he ask?")

An infinitive phrase is the word *to* plus a verb and its modifiers and/or direct object. Like the gerund, the infinitive, when used as a noun, retains the properties of a verb. For example, in the sentence

Dr. Gardiner decided to perform an exploratory operation immediately.

the words *to perform an exploratory examination immediately* make up an infinitive phrase answering the question "What did Dr. Gardiner decide?" The phrase contains the infinitive *to perform*, the direct object of the infinitive, *an exploratory operation;* and the adverbial modifier of the infinitive, *immediately.* The infinitive phrases in the following sentences are italicized.

To change an oil filter in an automobile is not a difficult task. (Subject of the sentence.)
Eleven students decided *to withdraw from the competition.* (Direct object answering the question "What did the students decide?")
Dr. Jones was the only professor who wanted *to eliminate compulsory class attendance.* (Direct object answering the question "What did Dr. Jones want?")
Ecologists want *to stop the pollution of rivers and streams.* (Direct object answering the question "What do ecologists want?")
Switzerland has managed *to remain neutral during the two major wars*

of this century. (Direct object answering the question "What has Switzerland managed?")

In addition to gerunds, gerund phrases, infinitives, and infinitive phrases, noun clauses can also be used as direct objects. A noun clause by definition is a group of words containing a subject and a predicate that is used as the subject of the sentence, the direct object, or anywhere a noun can be used in a sentence. For example, in the sentence

Professor Hirt knew that his students had not studied for the test.

that his students had not studied for the test is a group of words containing the subject *his students* and the predicate *had not studied for the test.* It is therefore a dependent clause, and in this sentence the clause is used to answer the question "What did Professor Hirt know?" It is therefore a noun clause used as the direct object. The noun clauses in the following sentences are italicized.

We knew *that our neighbor would feed our dog while we were gone.* (Direct object answering the question "What was known?")

The teacher promised *that he would dismiss us early.* (Direct object answering the question "What was promised?")

The queen said *that the people could eat cake.* (Direct object answering the question "What was said?")

What he knows about the case is a secret. (Subject of the sentence.)

I know *what the answer is.* (Direct object answering the question "What is known?")

EXERCISE 1
Compound Direct Objects

In this exercise you are to combine the sentences in each group into one sentence by using a compound direct object. Remember that the direct object can be a noun, a noun clause, a pronoun, an infinitive, an infinitive phrase, a gerund, or a gerund phrase. Again, when you have completed the exercise, turn to the section entitled "Suggested Answers" and examine one of the possible ways that each sentence group can be combined by using a compound direct object.

Group 1
1. For many years before the Europeans came to America, Indians had been growing corn and potatoes.
2. Indians had also been growing squash and beans before the Europeans came.

_____

_____

1. Some American Indians built huge burial mounds.
2. Other Indians built stone-faced pyramids.
3. Still others built limestone temples.

_____

_____

_____

1. The first Europeans believed that all Indians were uncivilized.
2. They also believed that all Indians looked alike.
3. Europeans also believed that all Indians were scalp hunters.

_____

_____

_____

1. The Indians tried to follow their tribal customs.
2. These Indians also tried to obey their tribal laws.

_____

_____

1. The terraced adobe houses of the Pueblo Indians had large rooms for food storage.
2. Underground rooms in these houses were used for religious ceremonies.
3. Apartments for hundreds of people were built into these Pueblo dwellings.

_____

_____

_____

1. Not a warlike people, the Pueblos wanted to live in peace.
2. Their primary concern was to tend their farms.
3. They also liked to weave colorful cloth of cotton and wool.

_____

_____

_____

1. The Apache Indians, a warlike tribe, fought and defeated the Spanish explorers.
2. They also fought and defeated the army troops of the United States.
3. American settlers were often attacked and defeated by the Apaches.

_____

_____

_____

LESSON 4: COMPOUND DIRECT OBJECTS / 41

Group 8   1. Europeans introduced smallpox, which wiped out thousands of Indians, to the New World.
2. Measles, a disease introduced by the white man, killed thousands of American Indians.
3. Other diseases introduced by Europeans were tuberculosis and influenza.

_____

_____

_____

Group 9   1. The typical Indian woman of the central plains wore deerskin moccasins and leggings.
2. Her dress was made in one piece and decorated with beads of many colors.

_____

_____

Group 10   1. The Indian warrior hunted deer for food.
2. Indians also depended on the wild buffalo for food.
3. Bear and moose were also eaten by Indians.

_____

_____

_____

Group 11   1. For traveling up and down rivers and streams, the Indians built birch-bark canoes.
2. Some Indians used elm bark in building their canoes.
3. Other Indians built boats of animal hide stretched over a wooden frame.

_____

_____

_____

Group 12   1. Some American Indians lived in grass houses.
2. Other Indians inhabited birch-bark tepees.
3. Still others lived in earth-covered hogans.

_____

_____

_____

Group 13   1. Indians in the South occupied raised dwellings roofed with palmetto leaves.
2. Other southern Indians lived in cabins built of logs.

_____

_____

Group 14   1. Some Indians used sleds drawn by dogs to transport goods.

2. Goods were also carried in baskets strapped to the backs of Indians.
3. A third method of transportation was the travois, made of long poles covered with skins and pulled by horses.

_____

_____

_____

1. Indians introduced succotash, a dish made of beans and corn, to the Pilgrims.   *Group 15*
2. The Pilgrims also learned from the Indians to eat baked beans.
3. Indians taught the Pilgrims to eat steamed clams.

_____

_____

_____

1. Some American Indians wore headpieces made of porcupine quills and animal hair.   *Group 16*
2. Other headgear worn by Indians was the war bonnet, fashioned of eagle feathers.
3. Still other Indians wore brightly colored cloth turbans.

_____

_____

_____

1. Indian warriors in the Northwest protected their bodies with wooden armor.   *Group 17*
2. These Indians also wore helmets made of carved wood.

_____

_____

1. Instead of metal, wood was used by Indians for tools.   *Group 18*
2. Indians also used animal bones to make tools.
3. Tools were also made of stone.

_____

_____

_____

1. Indian warriors included in their purification rites a potion that caused violent vomiting.   *Group 19*
2. These rites also included hot baths that caused intense sweating.
3. They washed their hair to expel evil spirits as part of the purification rites.

_____

_____

_____

Group 20 1. For recreation Indians played lacrosse.
2. They also played chenco.

_____

_____

When you have completed the exercise, write five original sentences
containing compound direct objects.

1. _____

_____

_____

2. _____

_____

_____

3. _____

_____

_____

4. _____

_____

_____

5. _____

_____

_____

EXERCISE 2
Compound Direct Objects

In this exercise you are again to combine the sentences in each group
into one sentence by using a compound direct object. Remember that
the direct object can be a noun, a pronoun, a noun clause, an infinitive, an infinitive phrase used as a noun, a gerund, or a gerund phrase.

Group 1 1. The state of California produces nine-tenths of the nation's
grapes.
2. One-fourth of the nation's sugar beets come from California.
3. Farmers in California grow one-tenth of the cotton produced
in the United States.

_____

_____

Group 2 1. Tourists in California can enjoy camping in national parks.
2. Many tourists visit California to enjoy fishing in mountain
streams.

3. Still other visitors in California surf in the waters of the Pacific Ocean.

_____

_____

_____

1. Traveling through the state of Montana, a visitor sees huge wheat farms.
2. He also sees large cattle ranches.
3. Tourists in Montana are often impressed by the many herds of sheep.

_____

_____

_____

Group 3

1. Montana produces much of the nation's copper.
2. More vermiculite is produced in Montana than in any other state in the Union.
3. Montana is also important in the production of petroleum.

_____

_____

_____

Group 4

1. The Missouri Compromise of 1820 decreed that the state of Maine be admitted to the United States as a free state.
2. This document also provided that Missouri be admitted as a slave state.

_____

_____

Group 5

1. During World War II Dwight D. Eisenhower helped to plan the invasion of North Africa.
2. During the same war Eisenhower was successful in directing the invasion of Europe.

_____

_____

Group 6

1. After World War II was over, Eisenhower became chief of staff for the United States armed forces.
2. Eisenhower later became president of Columbia University.
3. Still later he became president of the United States.

_____

_____

_____

Group 7

Group 8

1. William Shakespeare wrote great tragedies such as *Hamlet*.
2. Interesting historical plays such as *Richard III* were also written by Shakespeare.
3. Shakespeare was also responsible for such popular comedies as *As You Like It*.

_____

_____

_____

Group 9

1. John Milton, one of the greatest English authors, wrote the great literary epic *Paradise Lost*.
2. Milton also wrote the classical drama *Samson Agonistes*.
3. In the political tract *Areopagitica*, Milton denounced literary censorship.

_____

_____

_____

Group 10

1. One of Thomas Alva Edison's most significant inventions was the incandescent electric light bulb.
2. Edison's fame also rests on his invention of the phonograph.

_____

_____

Group 11

1. During World War II Field Marshall Viscount Montgomery led the forces that defeated Rommel in North Africa.
2. Later he led an army in the Italian Campaign.
3. His greatest achievement was his leadership of a military unit that participated in the invasion of France.

_____

_____

_____

Group 12

1. During his two terms as president of the United States, James Monroe supported the construction of the Erie Canal.
2. Monroe also favored the purchase of Florida from Spain.
3. Monroe supported the South American colonies that declared their independence from Spain.

_____

_____

_____

Group 13

1. Traditional educators believe that reading, writing, and arithmetic are the most important skills in the educational process.
2. For the traditionalist, courses such as speech and chorus are unnecessary parts of the school curriculum.

3. Typing, home economics, and agriculture are courses that the traditional educator frowns upon.

_____

_____

_____

1. Progressive educators favor student participation in curriculum planning.
2. They also support student-oriented rather than teacher-oriented classroom instruction.

Group 14

_____

_____

1. Tourists in Nevada can visit the copper mines at Ruth.
2. They can also enjoy a visit to Geyser Basin near Beowawe.
3. Visitors to Nevada can also see many ghost towns.

Group 15

_____

_____

_____

1. When he goes to New Mexico, the tourist can visit Carlsbad Caverns in the southwestern part of the state.
2. He can also visit Gila Forest in southeastern New Mexico.
3. Another interesting tourist attraction in New Mexico is the Taos art colony in the north central part of the state.

Group 16

_____

_____

_____

1. Farmers in Oklahoma find wheat to be the biggest cash crop in the state.
2. Cotton is second only to wheat as a cash crop in Oklahoma.

Group 17

_____

_____

1. A good dictionary contains a thorough definition of words.
2. The etymology, or history and derivation of words, is always included in a good dictionary.
3. To learn how a word is pronounced, a person can consult a good dictionary.

Group 18

_____

_____

_____

1. To find a synonym for a word, a student can consult a good dictionary.

Group 19

2. He can also consult a thesaurus in order to find a synonym for a word.

_____

_____

Group 20

1. To promote their children's education, parents should provide a good set of encyclopedias.

2. Parents should also see that there is a good dictionary in the home.

3. Parents should subscribe to a representative selection of good magazines.

_____

_____

_____

When you have completed this exercise, write five original sentences containing compound direct objects.

1. _____

_____

2. _____

_____

3. _____

_____

4. _____

_____

5. _____

_____

Compound Predicate Nominatives

THIS exercise is designed to provide practice in combining predicate nominatives in order to eliminate unnecessary words and thus improve your sentence structure. By definition a predicate nominative is a noun or pronoun that follows the predicate verb and means the same thing as the subject of the sentence. In other words, the predicate nominative identifies the subject of the sentence. In most cases the two parts of the sentence, the subject and the predicate nominative, can be substituted for each other without changing the meaning of the sentence. For example, in the sentence

Dr. Bonin is my English teacher.

Dr. Bonin is the subject of the sentence and *my English teacher* is the predicate nominative. It is apparent that the words *my English teacher* identify *Dr. Bonin* by telling who she is. Furthermore, the sentence could be written

My English teacher is Dr. Bonin.

In the sentence

Christopher Marlowe was a playwright.

Christopher Marlowe is the subject of the sentence and *a playwright* is the predicate nominative. Again, it is obvious that the words *a playwright* identify Christopher Marlowe by telling who he was. Again, the sentence could be written

A playwright was Christopher Marlowe.

The predicate nominatives in the following sentences are italicized.

During World War II Dwight D. Eisenhower was *Commander in Chief of the Allied European forces*.

In the Pacific Theater Douglas MacArthur was *the Commander in Chief*.

My major is *accounting*.

David Treen is *the governor of Louisiana*.

Wallace Stevens was *an American poet*.

The predicate nominative, like the direct object, can be a gerund, that is, it can be an *ing* form of the verb used as a noun. In the sentence

My favorite forms of recreation are swimming, water skiing, and canoeing.

the words *swimming, water skiing,* and *canoeing* are the *ing* forms of the verbs *swim, water ski,* and *canoe*. These words are used as nouns—in this sentence as predicate nominatives. Therefore, they are called gerunds. Notice that the subject of the sentence and the predicate nominatives can be reversed and the sentence written thus:

Swimming, water skiing, and canoeing are my favorite forms of recreation.

In the following sentences the gerunds functioning as predicate nominatives are italicized.

Two basic learning skills are *reading* and *writing*.

The basic mathematical skills are *adding, subtracting, multiplying,* and *dividing*.

John's favorite leisure-time activity is *reading*.

Diane's favorite sport is *fishing*.

Seeing is *believing*.

Similarly, gerund phrases can be used as predicate nominatives. A gerund phrase is an *ing* verb plus its modifiers and/or direct objects. For example, in the sentence

My father's favorite sport is hunting deer in Texas.

the phrase *hunting deer in Texas* is a gerund phrase. The word *hunting* is the gerund, that is, the *ing* verb used as a noun; the word *deer* is the direct object of the verb *hunting*; and the prepositional phrase *in Texas* is used as an adverbial modifier of the verb *hunting*. In this sentence the gerund phrase *hunting deer in Texas* follows the predicate verb *is* and means the same thing as the subject, *my father's favorite sport*. The sentence could be written

Hunting deer in Texas is my father's favorite sport.

In the following sentences the gerund phrases used as predicate nominatives are italicized.

> Professor Byrd's duties during registration are *advising English majors* and *working at the drop-add station*.
> My most tedious task during the fall semester was *writing a term paper*.
> The policeman's first assignment was *directing traffic at the football game*.
> Two basic writing skills are *writing good sentences* and *composing well-structured paragraphs*.
> One of my favorite summertime activities is *deepsea fishing off the coast of Florida*.

Just as infinitives and infinitive phrases can be used as direct objects, they can also be used as predicate nominatives. You probably remember from Lesson 4 that an infinitive can be defined as the word *to* plus a verb and that an infinitive phrase can be defined as an infinitive plus its modifiers and/or direct object. For example, *to sleep, to dream,* and *to drive* are all infinitives and can be used as predicate nominatives. In the sentence

> After a hard day's work, my one desire is to sleep.

the infinitive *to sleep* follows the verb *is* and identifies the subject *desire*. Therefore, it is an infinitive used as a predicate nominative. The infinitives used as predicate nominatives in the following sentences are italicized.

> My aim is *to succeed*.
> President Roth's purpose in coming before the group was *to resign*.
> The consensus was *to appeal*.
> My ambition is *to act*.
> Septian's only function on the football team is *to kick*.

An infinitive phrase can also be used as a predicate nominative. Look at the following sentence.

> After my parents bought our new Chrysler, my brother's favorite pastime was to drive the car slowly past his girl friend's house.

In the sentence the infinitive phrase *to drive the car slowly past his girlfriend's house* contains the infinitive *to drive;* the object of the infinitive, *the car;* the adverbial modifiers of the infinitive, *slowly;* and *past his girlfriend's house*. The phrase comes after the verb *was* and means the same thing as *pastime*. The phrase, therefore, is used as a predicate nominative. The infinitive phrases used as predicate nominatives in the following sentences are italicized.

The bane of my existence is *to be asked to subscribe to magazines.*
Horace's aim is *to write a Nobel Prize-winning novel.*
My purpose in this course is *to get you to write an error-free essay.*
Columbus' hope was *to discover a new route to India.*
Magellan's desire was *to circumnavigate the globe.*

In addition to gerunds, gerund phrases, infinitives, and infinitive phrases, noun clauses can also be used as predicate nominatives. A noun clause can be defined as a group of words containing a subject and a predicate verb that is used as a subject, a direct object, a predicate nominative, or anywhere a noun can be used in a sentence. Look at the following sentence.

What you say will be held against you.

The words *what you say* make up a clause containing the subject *you* and the verb *say*. The word group or clause is used as the subject of the verb *will be* and is therefore a noun clause. Look at the next sentence.

Your money is what I want.

In this sentence the dependent clause *what I want,* containing the subject *I* and the verb *want,* means the same thing as the subject *money.* Since the clause comes after the predicate verb *is,* it is a noun clause used as a predicate nominative. The noun clauses used as predicate nominatives in the following sentences are italicized.

The crucial thing is *what you intend to do about your grade.*
My solution is *that I report your conduct to the dean.*
The only other alternative is *that you report your conduct to the proper authorities.*
Your penalty may be *that you will be suspended for a semester.*
My hope is *that you have learned a valuable lesson from this experience.*

EXERCISE 1
Compound Predicate Nominatives

In this exercise you are to combine the sentences in each group into one sentence by using a compound predicate nominative. When you have completed the exercise, turn to the section entitled "Suggested Answers" and examine some of the possible ways the sentences can be combined.

Group 1   **1.** Konstantin E. Tsiolkovsky, a Russian scientist, was an important pioneer in the science of space travel.

2. Another pioneer in this field was an American, Robert H. Goddard.
3. The Hungarian-born German, Herman J. Oberth, explained in 1926 how rockets could be propelled into outer space.

_____
_____
_____

Group 2

1. The Mercury spacecraft, which carries one astronaut, is only one type of manned spacecraft developed by the United States.
2. The United States has also developed the Gemini spacecraft, which will carry two men.
3. The third type of spacecraft developed by the United States is called the Apollo, which carries three astronauts.

_____
_____
_____

Group 3

1. Manned spacecraft developed by Russia include the Vostok series, accommodating one cosmonaut.
2. The Russians also developed the Voskhod spacecraft, which holds three men.
3. The Soyuz space vehicle developed by the Russians carries four men.

_____
_____
_____

Group 4

1. Space probes, which travel to other parts of the solar system, include unmanned lunar spacecraft designed to study the moon.
2. Planetary probes, which collect and transmit information about other planets, are another type of space probes.
3. The interplanetary probes are space probes that go into orbit around the sun.

_____
_____
_____

Group 5

1. Alan B. Shepard, Jr., the first United States astronaut, rode the spacecraft Freedom 7.
2. The second United States astronaut, Virgil I. Grissom, made a suborbital flight in 1961.

3. John H. Glenn, Jr. rode Friendship 7, the first U.S. spacecraft to orbit the earth.

_____

_____

_____

Group 6
1. The first Russian cosmonaut was Yuri A. Gagarin, who orbited the earth in Vostok 1.
2. Gagarin was followed by Gherman S. Titov, who made seventeen earth orbits in one flight.

_____

_____

Group 7
1. Among the first men to travel to the moon was Neil Armstrong.
2. Michael Collins was with Armstrong in the lunar module.
3. The third man involved in the first moon landing was Edwin Aldrin.

_____

_____

_____

Group 8
1. One of the three Apollo spacecraft modules was the service module, which held the fuel tanks.
2. The command module housed the Apollo spacemen on their journey to and from the moon.
3. The part of the Apollo spacecraft that actually landed on the moon was called the lunar module.

_____

_____

_____

Group 9
1. One of the technical problems of space travel is overcoming the earth's gravity.
2. Staying in orbit is another problem facing space scientists.
3. The third major difficulty in space travel is how to get back to earth.

_____

_____

_____

Group 10
1. Russia is one of the only two countries in the world to have put man into orbit around the earth.
2. The other country is the United States.

_____

_____

1. Maracaibo is one of the largest lakes in South America.
2. Two other large South American lakes are Lake Patos and Lake Titicaca.

Group 11

_____   _____

_____

1. Precious stones produced in South America include emeralds mined in Colombia.
2. Diamonds are found in Brazil.

Group 12

_____

_____

1. One of the largest cities in South America is Sao Paulo, Brazil, which has a population of more than three million people.
2. Rio de Janeiro, also in Brazil, has a population of 3,300,000.
3. The third largest South American city is Buenos Aires, Argentina, with a population of 3,200,000.

Group 13

_____

_____

_____

1. Simon Bolivar helped the South Americans in their fight for independence from European domination.
2. Another leader in the fight for South American independence was José de San Martin.

Group 14

_____

_____

_____

1. One of the chief exports and sources of income in South America is the petroleum of Venezuela.
2. The many cattle exported from Argentina are important in the economy of South America.
3. Another source of wealth in South America is the copper industry of Peru.

Group 15

_____

_____

_____

_____

1. The official language of Brazil is Portuguese.
2. Spanish is spoken in the other nine countries of South America.

Group 16

_____

_____

LESSON 5: COMPOUND PREDICATE NOMINATIVES / 55

Group 17

1. People living in South America include Europeans and their descendents.
2. Native Indians make up part of the population.
3. Mixtures of Europeans and Indians called mestizos also live in South America.

_____

_____

_____

Group 18

1. One of the main objectives of present-day South American officials is to build more industries.
2. Officials also want to eradicate communicable diseases.
3. The improvement of education is a primary concern of all South American countries.

_____

_____

_____

Group 19

1. Christopher Columbus, sailing under the Spanish flag, was one of the first explorers to reach South America.
2. Soon after Columbus came to the New World, Francisco Pizarro claimed Peru for Spain.

_____

_____

Group 20

1. The Incas of Peru were a highly civilized people when the Europeans began their conquest of the New World.
2. Another highly civilized tribe that the first Europeans found in the New World were the Aztecs of Mexico.

_____

_____

_____

When you have combined all the sentences in this exercise, write five original sentences, each of which contains a compound predicate nominative.

1. _____

_____

_____

2. _____

_____

_____

3. _____

_____

_____

4. _____

5. _____
_____
_____
_____
_____

Compound Predicate Nominatives

Again in this exercise you are to combine the sentences in each group into one sentence by using a compound predicate nominative.

1. One of the three major fruit-growing areas in Canada is the Okanagan Valley in British Columbia.
2. Another fruit-growing area is the vineyards on the south-western shore of Lake Ontario.
3. Apples are grown in the Annapolis valley of Nova Scotia.

Group 1

_____
_____
_____

1. One of the largest railway systems in Canada is the government-owned Canadian National.
2. The other is the Canadian Pacific, which is a privately owned company.

Group 2

_____
_____

1. Important Canadian highways include the Alaskan Highway, which runs through British Columbia to the Yukon.
2. The Mackenzie Highway runs through Alberta to the Great Salt Lake.
3. Another important highway is the Trans-Canada Highway, which runs from the Pacific Ocean to the Atlantic Ocean.

Group 3

_____
_____
_____

1. Banff, one of the largest national parks in Canada, is located in Alberta and covers over a million acres.
2. Wood Buffalo National Park, containing 11,000,000 acres of land in Alberta and the Northwest Territories, is the largest national park in Canada.

Group 4

3. One other park, Jasper National Park, also in Alberta, includes over two million acres.

_____

_____

_____

Group 5

1. One of the major tourist attractions in Canada is the beautiful scenery.
2. Tourists are also attracted to the well-kept national parks.
3. Toronto and Quebec attract tourists who prefer vacations in the city.

_____

_____

_____

Group 6

1. Most of the people of Mexico live in the central plateau.
2. The rugged mountain area, where Mexico City is located, forms the second geographical area of Mexico.
3. A third geographical area is composed of the low plains along the Gulf of Mexico and the Gulf of California.

_____

_____

_____

Group 7

1. One of the climatic zones of Mexico is the *tierra caliente* of the coastal plains.
2. The *tierra templada* of the central plateau is the second climatic zone of Mexico.
3. The third climatic zone is the *tierra fria* of the mountain regions.

_____

_____

_____

Group 8

1. Mexico City is the site of the National Museum of Anthropology.
2. The National Museum of History is located in Mexico City.
3. The third Mexican museum, the National Gallery of Painting and Sculpture, can also be found in Mexico City.

_____

_____

_____

Group 9

1. Citlaltepetl, rising 18,701 feet above sea level, is the highest peak in Mexico.
2. The second highest peak in Mexico is Popocatepetl, which is 17,887 feet high.

3. Ixtacihuatl, 17,342 feet in height, is the third highest Mexican peak.

_____

_____

_____

1. Most Mexicans enjoy bullfights as a form of recreation. *Group 10*
2. Baseball is another national spectator sport.

_____

_____

1. The highest mountain peak in Central America is Tajumulco, *Group 11*
   which is 13,845 feet high.
2. Tacana, 13,428 feet in height, is the second highest peak in
   Central America.
3. The third highest mountain peak in Central America is the
   13,044-foot-high Acatenango.

_____

_____

_____

1. The population of Central America is composed largely of *Group 12*
   mestizos, a mixture of Indian and white blood.
2. Pure-blooded Indians are in the minority in Central America.
3. Another small segment of the population is composed of pure-
   blooded Spanish.

_____

_____

_____

1. The principal agricultural product of Central America is cof- *Group 13*
   fee.
2. Central America has large sugar cane plantations.
3. Many Central Americans own banana plantations.

_____

_____

_____

1. Edmonton is the capital of the Canadian province of Alberta. *Group 14*
2. Edmonton is also the largest city in Alberta.

_____

_____

1. Mt. McKinley, the highest mountain in the United States, is *Group 15*
   located in Alaska.
2. Another famous mountain, Mt. Everest, which is located on
   the Nepal–Tibet border, is the highest mountain in the world.

3. Mt. Logan, located in the Yukon Territory, is the highest mountain in Canada.

_____

_____

_____

Group 16   1. One of the primary aims of the medical profession is to prevent diseases.
2. Doctors also seek to cure diseases and to relieve suffering.

_____

_____

Group 17   1. The Mississippi River is the longest river in the United States.
2. This river is also the greatest commercial transport river in the world.

_____

_____

Group 18   1. One part of a microscope is the foot, which is the part on which the instrument rests.
2. Another part of a microscope is the tube, which holds the lenses.
3. Finally, there is the body, which contains the tube.

_____

_____

_____

Group 19   1. One of the two parts of the Olympic Games is the Summer Olympics.
2. The other part is the Winter Olympics.

_____

_____

Group 20   1. The woodwinds make up one section of a symphony orchestra.
2. Another section includes the percussion instruments.
3. The third section is the strings.
4. Finally, the fourth section includes the brass instruments.

_____

_____

_____

_____

When you have completed this exercise, write five original sentences containing compound predicate nominatives.

1. _____
   _____
   _____
2. _____
   _____
   _____
3. _____
   _____
   _____
4. _____
   _____
   _____
5. _____
   _____
   _____

Compound Adjectival Modifiers

THIS exercise provides practice in combining adjectival modifiers so that you can tighten your sentence structure and thus write more effectively. Combining such adjectival modifiers by using a series of adjectives in one sentence rather than writing a series of sentences, each of which provides a descriptive word modifying the same noun, enables you to eliminate unnecessary words.

By definition an adjective is a word that modifies a noun or pronoun. An easy way to identify adjectives is to find the words in a sentence that answer the questions "How many?" "Which one?" and "What kind?" That is, find the words that number, point out, or describe a noun or pronoun. For example, in the sentence

Several students failed to complete the exercise.

the word *several* answers the question "How many students failed to complete the exercise?" The word *several* thus numbers the students.

Furthermore, in the sentence

We are unable to accept those conditions.

the word *those* answers the question "Which ones?" or the question "Which conditions are we unable to accept?" Thus the word *those* points out.

By the same token, in the sentence

John asked his father for a pair of brown boots.

the word *brown* answers the question "For what kind of boots did John ask his father?" The word *brown* thus describes the boots.

Each of the three sentences that follow contains an adjective. Each of the three adjectives modifies the same noun.

Miss Brown washed her black hair.
Her hair is long.
Miss Brown's hair is straight.

If we look at the three sentences, we find three adjectives, *black, long,* and *straight,* that describe or tell what kind of hair Miss Brown has. These three adjectives can be put into one sentence.

Miss Brown washed her *long, straight, black* hair.

Thus we eliminate much repetition and tighten as well as strengthen our sentence structure.

Sometimes it is necessary to change a noun to an adjective in order to write one sentence rather than several sentences. For example, the three sentences that follow give some descriptive information about the streets of New Orleans.

I drove through the deserted streets of New Orleans.
The streets were wet.
They were strewn with litter.

In order to combine these three sentences and leave out no descriptive information, it is necessary to change the noun *litter* in the last sentence to the adjective *littered.* When this is done, the sentences can be combined thus:

I drove through the wet, littered, deserted streets of New Orleans.

By the same token, it is sometimes necessary to change a predicate adjective to a simple adjective. A predicate adjective is a descriptive or limiting word that follows the predicate verb and modifies or tells something about the simple subject. The three sentences that follow give descriptive information about the lectures Dr. Fields delivers.

Dr. Fields' lectures are always interesting.
His lectures are also concise.
Dr. Fields delivers stimulating lectures.

Notice that the adjectives *interesting* and *concise* follow the predicate verb *are* and describe the subject *lectures.* Thus, *concise* and *interesting* are predicate adjectives. In order to combine these three sentences, it is necessary to change these two predicate adjectives to simple adjectives.

Dr. Fields delivers interesting, concise, and stimulating lectures.

On the other hand, simple adjectives can be changed to predicate adjectives to achieve the same result.

Dr. Fields' lectures are always interesting, concise, and stimulating.

The same processes can be used to tighten the structure of the following three sentences.

A police car siren heard in the dead of night has an ominous sound.
This sound is eerie.
It is also frightening.

The three adjectives *ominous, eerie,* and *frightening* can be used as predicate adjectives modifying the subject *sound.*

The sound of a police car siren heard in the middle of the night is ominous, eerie, and frightening.

However, in this sentence, simple adjectives can also be used, and such use perhaps results in a sentence that has a better sound.

A police car siren heard in the middle of the night has an ominous, eerie, and frightening sound.

EXERCISE 1
Compound Adjectival Modifiers

In the following exercise you are to combine the sentences in each group by writing one sentence that contains a compound adjectival modifier. Again, when you have completed the exercise, refer to the section entitled "Suggested Answers" and examine one of the possible ways each sentence group can be combined into one sentence.

Group 1
1. The breathtaking scenery of Scotland includes the barren mountain peaks of the Western Highlands.
2. These mountain peaks are rugged and windswept.

_____

_____

Group 2
1. Loch Lomond is the most beautiful of Scotland's numerous lakes.
2. It is also the largest lake in Scotland.
3. Loch Lomond is also considered Scotland's most celebrated lake.

_____

_____

_____

Group 3
1. Scotland's heritage is reflected in its many ancient castles.
2. These castles are well preserved.

3. They are also spectacularly beautiful.

_____

_____

_____

1. Tiny villages dot Scotland's landscape. *Group 4*
2. These villages are peaceful and picturesque.

_____

_____

1. The Wicklow Mountain area of Ireland is a remote region of *Group 5*
enormous forests and winding streams.
2. It is a solitary and awesome region.

_____

_____

1. One of the most colorful regions of Ireland is Connemara. *Group 6*
2. This is an isolated region.
3. It is also a romantic area.

_____

_____

_____

1. England's Stonehenge is a unique collection of stone pillars. *Group 7*
2. These mysterious prehistoric pillars are thought to be the
remnants of ancient temples built by sun worshippers.

_____

_____

1. An event that takes place in Ireland in early August is the *Group 8*
Dublin Horse Show.
2. This annual show is an international event.

_____

_____

1. One of England's favorite tourist excursions is a motor trip *Group 9*
through the lush countryside to Windsor Castle.
2. The countryside is sparsely settled.

_____

_____

1. Many tourists think France is an interesting country. *Group 10*
2. Others enjoy the beauty of the country.
3. Still others remember France as a colorful country.

_____

_____

_____

Group 11   **1.** Paris is the largest city in France.
            2. Frenchmen are proud of the charm and beauty of this city, which is their country's capital.

_____

_____

Group 12   **1.** Frenchmen are well known for their independence.
            2. They work hard.
            3. They are also thrifty.

_____

_____

_____

Group 13   **1.** Notre Dame Cathedral, located in Paris, is a magnificent example of medieval Gothic architecture.
            2. It is a world-renowned example of this type of architecture.

_____

_____

Group 14   **1.** Sidewalk cafés are the social centers of Paris.
            2. These cafés are popular with the young and old alike.
            3. Tourists also enjoy these picturesque cafés.

_____

_____

_____

Group 15   **1.** Many Bretons, occupying the northwestern part of France, are seafaring people.
            2. These people are unusually industrious.
            3. They are also frugal.

_____

_____

_____

_____

Group 16   **1.** Many chateaux, or mansions, that dot the French countryside were the feudal citadels of French landlords.
            2. These chateaux were moat-surrounded fortresses.
            3. They were relatively impregnable.

_____

_____

_____

_____

Group 17   **1.** Today many of these chateaux are well-preserved tourist attractions.

2. They are maintained by the French government.

_____

_____

1. One of the architectural phenomena of France is the famous Abbey of Mont St. Michel.

2. This island monastery was built in medieval times.

_____

_____

Group 18

1. Among the most popular French resorts is the French Riviera, located on the Mediterranean coast.

2. The French Riviera is an internationally known gathering place for the world's jet set.

_____

_____

Group 19

1. In southeastern France the tourist meets the swarthy Basques of the Pyrenees Mountains.

2. Basques are a fiercely independent people.

3. Their independence is combined with unusual courage.

_____

_____

_____

Group 20

When you have completed this exercise, write five original sentences containing compound adjectival modifiers.

1. _____

_____

_____

2. _____

_____

_____

3. _____

_____

_____

4. _____

_____

_____

5. _____

_____

_____

EXERCISE 2
Compound Adjectival Modifiers

In this exercise you are to combine the sentences in each group into one sentence by using a compound adjectival modifier.

Group 1
1. The gazelle is a slender animal of the antelope family.
2. The gazelle is considered one of the fastest and most graceful of all animals.

_____

_____

_____

Group 2
1. The gnu, or wildebeest, is an African antelope.
2. It is a rather peculiar-looking animal.
3. The gnu is a large animal.

_____

_____

_____

Group 3
1. Another animal of the antelope family, the eland, also lives in Africa.
2. The eland, unlike the gnu, is a slow-moving animal.
3. The eland is also docile.

_____

_____

_____

Group 4
1. The giraffe is native to Africa.
2. This animal moves swiftly.
3. It is extremely tall.

_____

_____

_____

Group 5
1. Elephants, which are native to both Africa and Asia, are grey in color.
2. These animals are thick-skinned.
3. Elephants are larger than any other land animal.

_____

_____

_____

Group 6
1. The gibbon is a small ape.
2. It has no tail.

3. The gibbon is native to Asia.

_____

_____

_____

1. The aardvark lives in Africa.
2. It is a nocturnal animal; that is, it moves about at night and sleeps during the day.
3. Its principal food is the ant.

_____

_____

_____

Group 7

1. In Australia one can find a wild dog called the dingo.
2. The dingo is a medium-sized animal.
3. It is carnivorous; that is, it eats meat rather than plants.

_____

_____

_____

Group 8

1. The cacomistle is a fur-bearing animal.
2. It is a carnivorous animal native to Mexico.
3. It resembles the raccoon.

_____

_____

_____

Group 9

1. Gannets are large birds.
2. They are white in color.
3. They eat fish.

_____

_____

_____

Group 10

1. The tuatara lives on islands near the New Zealand coast.
2. It resembles the lizard.
3. It is a large, spiny quadruped.

_____

_____

_____

Group 11

1. The chevrotain is a small, goatlike animal native to Asia and Africa.
2. It is a ruminating animal; that is, it chews its cud.

_____

_____

_____

Group 12

Group 13   1. Tapirs are large animals.
             2. They are ungalates; that is, they have hooves.
             3. Harmless in nature, the tapir is generally nocturnal.

             _____

             _____

             _____

Group 14   1. Tarantulas are hairy spiders native to Europe but found in many other parts of the world.
             2. These large spiders are sluggish in nature.

             _____

             _____

Group 15   1. The badger is a burrowing animal.
             2. It is carnivorous.
             3. A nocturnal animal, the badger can be found in North America, Europe, and Asia.

             _____

             _____

             _____

Group 16   1. The caribou is a herbivorous animal; that is, it eats plant life rather than meat.
             2. It is a wild animal of the reindeer family.
             3. The caribou is native to North America.

             _____

             _____

             _____

Group 17   1. The coati is a small, raccoonlike animal.
             2. It has a bushy tail and a long nose.
             3. The coati is native to Latin America.

             _____

             _____

             _____

Group 18   1. The mongoose is a fast-moving animal native to India.
             2. In size the mongoose resembles the ferret.
             3. The mongoose feeds on snakes.

             _____

             _____

             _____

Group 19   1. Sloths are arboreal animals; that is, they live in trees.
             2. They are herbivorous rather than carnivorous.

3. Sloths are sluggish animals.

_____

_____

_____

1. Hyenas are large, carnivorous quadrupeds; that is, they have four legs.
2. These animals operate chiefly at night; thus, they are nocturnal.

_____

_____

When you have completed this exercise, write five original sentences containing compound adjectival modifiers.

1. _____

_____

_____

2. _____

_____

_____

3. _____

_____

_____

4. _____

_____

_____

5. _____

_____

_____

Compound Adverbial Modifiers

THIS lesson is designed to help you write more effectively and concisely by using compound adverbial modifiers. Combining adverbial modifiers by using a series of adverbs in one sentence rather than writing a series of sentences, each of which contains an adverb modifying the same verb, adjective, or adverb, enables you to eliminate unnecessary words and thus tighten your sentence structure by writing more concisely.

By definition an adverb is a word that modifies a verb, an adjective, or another adverb. An easy way to determine which word or words in a sentence are adverbs is to find the word that answers one of the questions "How?" "When?" or "Where?" That is, find the words that indicate manner, time, and place.

For example, in the sentence

The policeman walked cautiously down the alley.

the word *cautiously* answers the question "How did the policeman walk?" It is therefore an adverb indicating manner.

Likewise, in the sentence

Mr. Pendergrast, who has a heart condition, must go to the doctor periodically.

the word *periodically* answers the question "When does Mr. Pendergrast have to go to the doctor?" The word *periodically* is, therefore, an adverb indicating time.

Furthermore, in the sentence

The interior decorator wants the grandfather clock placed here.

the word *here* answers the question "Where does the interior decorator want the clock placed?" The word *here* is, therefore, an adverb indicating place.

In each of the two sentences that follow, there is an adverb. Each of the two adverbs modifies the same verb.

> Jennifer quickly completed the paperwork necessary for the transfer of the property.
> She completed this work satisfactorily.

In the first sentence the word *quickly* tells how Jennifer completed the paperwork. In the second sentence the word *satisfactorily* also tells how she completed the work. The two sentences can be combined by using a compound adverb.

> Jennifer quickly and satisfactorily completed the paperwork necessary for the transfer of the property.

Sometimes it is necessary to change an adjective to an adverb in order to combine two sentences into one sentence containing a compound adverb. For example, in the second of the two sentences that follow,

> My secretary frequently intrudes upon my privacy.
> These intrusions are regular.

the adjective *regular* can be changed to the adverb *regularly* and then the two sentences can be combined into one sentence containing a compound adverb.

> My secretary frequently and regularly intrudes upon my privacy.

Both *regularly* and *frequently* indicate time; that is, they tell when the secretary intrudes upon my privacy.

EXERCISE 1
Compound Adverbial Modifiers

In the following exercise you are to combine the sentences in each group into one sentence containing a compound adverbial modifier. When you have completed the exercise, turn to the answer section and examine one of the possible ways each group of sentences can be written as one sentence.

Group 1

1. The guide reluctantly led the tourists into the underground cavern.
2. In spite of his reluctance, he was gracious in his manner.

_____

_____

Group 2

1. One of the tourists said emphatically that he would go no farther.

2. He made this announcement in a loud voice.

_____

_____

Group 3   1. The frightened tourist had learned that the floor of the cave was gradually disappearing.
2. He had also heard that the disappearance was mysterious.

_____

_____

Group 4   1. Everyone in the group quickly demanded that the tour be canceled.
2. Their voices were forceful as they made the demand.

_____

_____

Group 5   1. The guide eagerly suggested that the tourists explore the ancient ruins above ground.
2. His suggestion was immediate.

_____

_____

Group 6   1. The guide told us that the Aztec Indians easily conquered the native tribes of central Mexico.
2. The conquest was complete, he added.

_____

_____

Group 7   1. After the conquest the Aztecs slowly created a magnificent empire.
2. They were patient in this slow endeavor.

_____

_____

Group 8   1. In 1519 the Aztecs, in turn, were ruthlessly conquered by Hernando Cortez, a Spaniard who came to the New World in search of gold.
2. This conquest, too, was complete.

_____

_____

Group 9   1. Cortez virtually enslaved the Aztecs.
2. This enslavement occurred soon after his arrival.

_____

_____

1. For four hundred years the people of Mexico stoically endured domination by greedy and unscrupulous administrators.
2. Although they were stoic, they were resentful.

Group 10

_____

_____

1. During those four centuries several unsuccessful attempts were made by a few leaders to establish a democratic form of government.
2. These attempts, though unsuccessful, reflected great courage on the part of the leaders.

Group 11

_____

_____

1. Finally, in 1924, Plutarco Elías Calles was elected president.
2. Calles' election was a fortunate one for the Mexican peasants.

Group 12

_____

_____

1. Calles was relentless in the expropriation of large tracts of land.
2. Calles systematically confiscated this land, which was owned by a few wealthy Mexican families and foreign investors.

Group 13

_____

_____

1. These large tracts of land were divided equally among more than two million Mexican families.
2. The land was given to communities as well as to individuals.

Group 14

_____

_____

1. Proud of their new ownership, the Mexican peasants worked long hours to make their farms successful.
2. The families worked more diligently for themselves than they had for the wealthy landowners.

Group 15

_____

_____

1. In the last fifty years, as a result of land reform, the standard of living in Mexico has risen dramatically.
2. The rise has been a continuous one.

Group 16

_____

_____

Group 17   **1.** In spite of such rapid reform, about half of Mexico's population is still very poor.

        2. This half lives dangerously near and below poverty level.

        _____

        _____

Group 18   **1.** Thousands of poverty-stricken Mexicans ultimately emigrate to the United States.

        2. These emigrants enter the United States illegally.

        _____

        _____

Group 19   **1.** The United States Immigration Service conscientiously attempts to halt such illegal entry.

        2. They have thus far been unsuccessful.

        _____

        _____

Group 20   **1.** Both the Mexican and American governments have worked untiringly to institute workable immigration and emigration policies.

        2. Their attempts have been fruitless.

        _____

        _____

When you have completed this exercise, write five original sentences containing compound adverbial modifiers.

1. _____

_____

_____

2. _____

_____

_____

3. _____

_____

_____

4. _____

_____

_____

5. _____

_____

_____

Compound Adverbial Modifiers

In the following exercise you are to combine the sentences in each group into one sentence containing more than one adverbial modifier.

1. Although the author worked slowly, he eventually completed the manuscript.
2. The manuscript was quite satisfactorily written.

Group 1

_____

_____

1. In his most recent book Norman Ellison eloquently defends the construction of nuclear power plants.
2. His defense, although eloquent, is cautious.

Group 2

_____

_____

_____

1. Opponents of nuclear power plant construction almost immediately criticized Ellison's argument.
2. Their criticism was severe.

Group 3

_____

_____

_____

1. His opponents openly condemned Ellison as an antihumanitarian.
2. Their anger was apparent.

Group 4

_____

_____

1. Antinuclear demonstrators bluntly demanded that Ellison's book be banned.
2. They were emphatic in their demand.

Group 5

_____

_____

1. Ellison quickly defended his position.
2. His defense was quietly offered.

Group 6

_____

_____

1. He argued convincingly that the only solution to the energy problem was the immediate expansion of nuclear facilities.

Group 7

2. His argument was, in many respects, correct.

_____

_____

Group 8 **1.** Ellison said that if nuclear plants were periodically examined, there would be no danger of radiation for inhabitants of areas surrounding the plants.
2. He also said that the examinations had to be carefully carried out.

_____

_____

Group 9 **1.** Supporters of nuclear energy will eventually be victorious.
2. Their eventual victory is obvious.

_____

_____

Group 10 **1.** Fundamentally, reliance on foreign oil is unfeasible.
2. Such reliance is not economically sound.

_____

_____

Group 11 **1.** The Middle Eastern countries could suddenly curtail oil exportation to the United States.
2. Such a cutback in Middle Eastern oil exportation to the United States could be severe.

_____

_____

Group 12 **1.** Wind power is now being used successfully as a source of power.
2. Such wind power is economical.

_____

_____

Group 13 **1.** Solar power will eventually alter the demand for petroleum.
2. The decreased demand for petroleum resulting from the use of solar energy will be significant.

_____

_____

Group 14 **1.** A significant amount of energy is wasted in homes because of attic and window leaks, which could easily be eliminated.
2. These leaks could be eliminated cheaply.

_____

_____

1. With technological advancement, the cost of geothermal energy will eventually be reduced.
2. This cost reduction will be great.

Group 15

_____

_____

1. A quick and permanent solution to the energy problem is highly unlikely.
2. It is apparent to everyone that the energy problem will not be solved quickly and permanently.

Group 16

_____

_____

1. A program of energy conservation must be vigorously pursued.
2. The policy of energy conservation must be permanent.

Group 17

_____

_____

1. Research projects by private industries could be substantially expanded.
2. Such an expansion would be a permanent one.

Group 18

_____

_____

1. Many people feel that the federal government is steadily escalating its role in energy research.
2. This escalation, they feel, is largely unintentional.

Group 19

_____

_____

1. An alternate source of cheap and plentiful energy will, no doubt, eventually be found.
2. The discovery will probably be quite accidental.

Group 20

_____

_____

After you have completed this exercise, write five original sentences using a compound adverbial modifier.

1. _____

_____

_____

2. _____

_____

_____

3. _____
_____
_____

4. _____
_____
_____

5. _____
_____
_____

Combining Sentences by Using Participial Phrases

HIS lesson is designed to familiarize you with participial phrases and to show how the use of such phrases can improve sentence structure and thus improve your writing.

By definition a participial phrase is an *ing* or *ed* form of the verb (past participles of irregular verbs are in forms other than the *-ed* form; i.e., *chosen* is the past participle of the verb *choose*) plus its object and any accompanying modifiers. The participial phrase functions as an adjective in the sentence by modifying a noun or pronoun—that is, by describing, limiting, or pointing out a noun or pronoun. For example, in the sentence

> The doctor attending my husband is a graduate of Johns Hopkins University.

the phrase *attending my husband* is made up of the *ing* verb *attending* plus its object *husband* and the possessive pronoun *my*. The phrase answers the question "Which doctor is a graduate of Johns Hopkins University?" and thus functions as an adjective by pointing out the particular doctor.

Again, in the sentence

> St. Paul's Cathedral, designed by Christopher Wren and built after the great London fire of 1666, is considered one of the most magnificent structures in England.

the two phrases

> designed by Christopher Wren
> built after the great London fire of 1666

are participial phrases that further describe St. Paul's Cathedral. The first phrase, *designed by Christopher Wren*, is made up of the *ed* verb *designed* and its modifier *by Christopher Wren*. The second phrase, *built after the great London fire of 1666,* is made up of the participle *built* (past participle of the irregular verb *build*) and its modifiers. Both phrases are introduced by past participles and give additional descriptive information about St. Paul's Cathedral.

The use of such participial phrases often enables you to be more concise in expressing yourself. Superfluous words can be eliminated and sentence structure can be more varied and interesting. For example, the two sentences

The man wore a swan costume to the ball.
He won the prize for the most original costume.

can be combined into one sentence by changing *wore a swan costume* to a participial phrase, *dressed as a swan,* and writing

The man dressed as a swan won the prize for the most original costume at the ball.

Furthermore, the two sentences

Griffin Hall was built in 1974.
It is the newest building on campus.

can be combined by simply eliminating the word *was* in the first sentence.

Griffin Hall, built in 1974, is the newest building on campus.

Thus, *built in 1974* becomes a participial phrase describing Griffin Hall.

It is also possible to condense adjective clauses into participial phrases and thereby tighten sentence structure. For example, the sentence

I have just completed the 1981 Pulitzer Prize-winning novel, which was written by Ken Toole.

can be condensed by changing the adjective clause *which was written by Ken Toole* to a participial phrase, *written by Ken Toole.* The sentence then reads

I have recently completed the 1981 Pulitzer Prize-winning novel written by Ken Toole.

Although the use of participial phrases can result in better writing, you should use caution in beginning a sentence with a participial phrase. You must be certain that such an introductory participial phrase modifies the subject of the sentence. For example, in the sentence

Looking through his field glasses, the hummingbird was sighted by the ornithologist.

the introductory participial phrase dangles; that is, it does not modify *hummingbird*. The sentence can be correctly written thus:

> Looking through his field glasses, the ornithologist sighted the hummingbird.

Combining Sentences by Using Participial Phrases

Each of the following groups of sentences is to be combined into one sentence by using a participial phrase. When you have completed the exercise, turn to the section entitled "Suggested Answers" and examine one of the possible ways the sentences can be combined by using a participial phrase.

Group 1
1. Switzerland is often called the playground of Europe.
2. Switzerland attracts tourists from all over the world.

_____

_____

Group 2
1. The Swiss people are motivated by a strong desire for freedom.
2. They have a truly democratic form of government.

_____

_____

Group 3
1. Three official languages are spoken by the Swiss people.
2. They are German, French, and Italian.

_____

_____

Group 4
1. The Rhaeto–Romantic language is spoken in only one canton.
2. This tongue is similar to Latin.

_____

_____

Group 5
1. The president of Switzerland is elected by the Federal Assembly for one year.
2. He cannot immediately succeed himself.

_____

_____

Group 6   1. Railroads tunnel through the mountains of Switzerland.
2. These railroads make year-round travel possible.

_____

_____

Group 7   1. The Mittelland Plateau lies between the Jura Mountains on the north and the Alps on the south.
2. This plateau is one of the principal land routes of central Europe.

_____

_____

Group 8   1. In Bern, Switzerland, tourists can wander leisurely up and down quaint winding streets.
2. These streets are lined with picturesque little houses built of green and yellow limestone.

_____

_____

Group 9   1. In Lucerne the tourist is encouraged to explore the medieval Mill Bridge.
2. Mill Bridge is decorated with grim scenes of the Dance of Death.

_____

_____

Group 10   1. The city of Brienz is known worldwide for its beautiful and unique wood carvings.
2. Brienz attracts many tourists to Switzerland every year.

_____

_____

Group 11   1. Lake Lucerne is surrounded by beautiful forests and snow-capped mountains.
2. This lake offers some of the most breathtaking scenery in Switzerland.

_____

_____

Group 12   1. Quaint little villages huddle against the spectacular Swiss mountains.
2. These villages provide quiet, peaceful inns for the exhausted tourist.

_____

_____

1. San Moritz is often referred to as the Queen of the Alps.
2. Many resort homes of San Moritz are occupied by royalty and millionaires.

Group 13

_____

_____

1. Chillon Castle was immortalized by the English poet Byron in "The Prisoner of Chillon."
2. This castle is located on the edge of Lake Geneva.

Group 14

_____

_____

1. "The Prisoner of Chillon" was based on the life of François de Bonnivard.
2. The poem is largely fictional rather than factual.

Group 15

_____

_____

1. The distant Alps frame the cobalt blue waters of the Lake of the Four Forest Canons.
2. This scene is one of unsurpassed beauty.

Group 16

_____

_____

1. A trip to Switzerland would be incomplete without a visit to Montreux.
2. Montreux is situated on the shores of Lake Geneva.

Group 17

_____

_____

1. In Lucerne the tourist can enjoy a spectacular view of the Alps by taking a ride on the cable car.
2. The cable car extends to the top of Mount Rigi.

Group 18

_____

_____

1. Tourists are impressed by the warmth and hospitality of the Swiss people.
2. They often plan to make a return trip to this fabulously beautiful country.

Group 19

_____

_____

1. Switzerland nestles between France and Germany.
2. It has been strangely free from war for more than a century.

Group 20

LESSON 8: COMBINING SENTENCES BY USING PARTICIPIAL PHRASES / 85

Now write five original sentences containing participial phrases.

1. _____
_____
_____

2. _____
_____
_____

3. _____
_____
_____

4. _____
_____
_____

5. _____
_____
_____
_____

EXERCISE 2
Combining Sentences by Using Participial Phrases

Each of the following groups of sentences is to be combined into one sentence containing a participial phrase.

Group 1
1. The Pyramids of Egypt are built of stones weighing over two tons.
2. The Pyramids are architectural wonders.

_____
_____

Group 2
1. The Pyramids were built to house the tombs of the pharaohs of ancient Egypt.
2. The Pyramids are visited by thousands of tourists each year.

_____
_____

Group 3
1. The Sphinx faces the rising sun.
2. It seems to guard the Pyramids.

_____
_____

1. One tomb is that of the boy pharaoh Tutankhamun.
2. It is the only one that has not been disturbed by robbers.

_____

_____

1. Among the treasures found in King Tutankhamun's tomb are beautiful alabaster vases.
2. These vases are intricately decorated with priceless precious stones.

_____

_____

1. The treasures also include King Tut's wooden shrine.
2. This shrine is surrounded by exquisite golden statues.

_____

_____

1. At Saqqara, near Memphis, tourists can visit the famous Step Pyramid.
2. The Step Pyramid was designed by Imhotep and is believed to be the oldest freestanding stone structure in the world.

_____

_____

1. The mastaba, or tomb, of Mereruka is also located at Saqqara.
2. It contains over thirty chambers or rooms.

_____

_____

1. About three hundred miles south of Saqqara is the huge complex of temples at Karnak.
2. This complex covers about sixty acres.

_____

_____

1. The Luxor Temple was once connected with Karnak by the two-mile-long Avenue of the Sphinxes.
2. This temple was built in the fourteenth century B.C.

_____

_____

1. The Great Temple of Amun is the largest hypostyle hall in the world.
2. It covers an area of 50,000 square feet.

_____

_____

Group 13

1. Many people consider the Karnak Temple complex the most impressive archaeological site in the world.
2. This complex is one of the most popular tourist attractions in Egypt.

_____

_____

Group 14

1. The Temple of Sethos I is located in Abydos, ninety miles west of Karnak.
2. It was built to honor the god Osiris.

_____

_____

Group 15

1. The wall decorations of the Temple of Sethos I represent Egyptian art at its peak.
2. These decorations are dainty and fragile.

_____

_____

Group 16

1. The Temple of Hathor at Dendera is decorated with drawings of the signs of the zodiac.
2. This temple was built in the first century B.C.

_____

_____

Group 17

1. Sixty-four tombs of pharaohs have been found at the necropolis of ancient Thebes.
2. This necropolis is known as the Valley of the Kings and Queens.

_____

_____

Group 18

1. The New High Dam at Aswan is the largest landfill dam in the world.
2. It was built to curb the annual flooding of the Nile River.

_____

_____

Group 19

1. The colossal Temple of Abu Simbel was built in 1200 B.C.
2. This gigantic temple was hewn out of solid rock.

_____

_____

Group 20

1. Four colossal statues of Rameses II adorn the entry of the Great Hypostyle Hall.
2. These statues are flanked by the king's royal family.

Now write five original sentences containing participial phrases.

1. _____
   _____
   _____

2. _____
   _____
   _____

3. _____
   _____
   _____

4. _____
   _____
   _____

5. _____
   _____
   _____

Compound Gerunds and Gerund Phrases

THIS lesson is designed to acquaint you with gerunds and gerund phrases and to show how they can be used effectively in the construction of good sentences.

A gerund can be defined as the *ing* form of the verb functioning as a noun. A gerund phrase is the gerund plus its objects and modifiers. These gerunds or gerund phrases can function as subjects, as direct objects, as predicate nouns, as objects of prepositions, or as any other part of the sentence where a noun can be used. For example, in the sentence

Seeing is believing.

the gerund *seeing* is the subject of the verb *is* and the predicate noun is the gerund *believing*. Both words are *ing* verbs used as nouns. Again, in the sentence

Writing a good essay can be a difficult task for many beginning college students.

the subject of the verb *can be* is the gerund phrase *writing a good essay*. The phrase, made up of the *ing* verb *writing* plus its object *essay* and the modifiers *a* and *good,* is used as a noun.

In the sentence

I always lock the doors before leaving the house.

leaving the house, a phrase made up of the *ing* verb *leaving,* its object *house,* and the modifier *the,* is used as the object of the preposition *before.*

Furthermore, in the sentence

Helen dreaded going home alone.

the gerund phrase *going home alone,* made up of the *ing* verb *going* plus the object *home* and the modifier *alone,* is used as the direct object of the verb *dreaded,* telling what Helen dreaded.

Frequently the information offered in a series of two or three sentences can be condensed into one sentence by formulating gerund phrases that contain the information. For example, the two sentences

Helen dreaded going home alone.
She was afraid that she would find an intruder.

can be combined into one sentence containing a compound gerund phrase. To accomplish this, the information offered in the second sentence can be incorporated into the gerund phrase *finding an intruder.* The two sentences can thus be combined into one sentence containing a compound gerund phrase.

Helen dreaded going home alone and finding an intruder.

Furthermore, in the two sentences

Snow skiing is one of my two favorite sports.
The other sport I enjoy most is hang gliding.

can be condensed into one sentence by using the gerund *hang gliding* as part of a compound subject and writing the sentence thus:

Snow skiing and hang gliding are my two favorite sports.

The two sentences can also be combined by using the two gerunds *snow skiing* and *hang gliding* as predicate nouns.

The two sports I enjoy most are snow skiing and hang gliding.
My two favorite sports are snow skiing and hang gliding.

Combining sentences by using compound gerunds or gerund phrases is yet another way to eliminate unnecessary words from your writing and thus tighten your sentence and paragraph structure.

EXERCISE 1

Compound Gerunds and Gerund Phrases

Each of the following groups of sentences is to be combined into one sentence containing a compound gerund or a compound gerund phrase. It will be necessary in some instances to completely change the wording of one or both of the sentences in order to put the necessary information into a gerund or a gerund phrase. When you have completed the exercise, refer to the section entitled "Suggested Answers" and examine one of the possible ways that each sentence group can be combined into one sentence by using gerunds or gerund phrases.

Group 1
1. Salmon and trout fishing lure visitors to Argentina's Lake District.
2. The tourist can also enjoy skiing and mountain climbing in the Lake District of Argentina.

_____

_____

Group 2
1. Visitors to Buenos Aires enjoy strolling along Avenida 9 de Julio, the widest boulevard in the world.
2. These tourists also like to visit Plaza de Mayo, the city's heart and the birthplace of Argentine independence.

_____

_____

Group 3
1. Drinking tea at a *confeteria* on Calle Florida is a gustatory delight for the tourist in Buenos Aires.
2. Tourists in Buenos Aires can also savor the excellent charcoal-broiled steaks at La Cabaña.

_____

_____

Group 4
1. The tourist should not leave South America without visiting the jungle area on the Argentina–Brazil border.
2. Here he can explore the two-and-a-half-mile-wide Iguassa Falls.

_____

_____

Group 5
1. An exciting side trip for the visitor to Rio de Janeiro is taking the cable car to the top of Sugarloaf Mountain.
2. Another exciting side trip is a drive through Tijuca Rain Forest to Corcovado Peak.

_____

_____

Group 6
1. The tourist interested in early South American civilization should spend part of a day examining the Incan baths at Tambomachay.
2. The rest of the day could be devoted to an exploration of the Incan fortress at Sacsahuaman.

_____

_____

1. A morning in Lima can be spent shopping for gold and silver, ceramics, and woolens.
2. Such a morning should also include a visit to the Cathedral on Plaza de Armas, where the remains of Pizarro lie.

Group 7

_____

_____

1. A visit to the Amazon Safari Camp begins with a flight from Lima to Iquitos.
2. The visitor to this safari camp must travel by motorboat twenty miles down the Amazon River.

Group 8

_____

_____

1. The tourist can also fly east from Lima to the Island of Baltra, where he can board a yacht.
2. The yacht will take him on a cruise of the Galapagos Islands.

Group 9

_____

_____

1. A cruise of the Galapagos Islands offers a variety of experiences, such as talking with the scientists at the Charles Darwin Research Station.
2. The cruise also includes a chance to observe the sea lion nurseries on South Plaza Island.

Group 10

_____

_____

_____

1. A visit to James Island in the Galapagos offers the opportunity of seeing the remains of an old salt mine.
2. On James Island the tourist can also photograph a colony of fur seals.

Group 11

_____

_____

1. In Ecuador the tourist should insist on a visit to Quito, the national capital.
2. In Quito he should see the Equatorial Monument and La Compania Cathedral.

Group 12

_____

_____

1. A motor trip from Quito south to Latacunga offers the tourist the opportunity of driving through the Valley of Volcanoes.

Group 13

2. Here he can observe many unusual rock formations.

_____

_____

Group 14   1. Tourists in Bogota, the capital of Colombia, enjoy visiting the famous Gold Museum.
2. Ascending Monserrate Mountain in a cable car is a must for the visitor to Bogota.

_____

_____

Group 15   1. Watching a good soccer game can be an exciting event for the tourist in Cartagena, Colombia.
2. Tourists in Cartagena may prefer to relax on the sun-bathed beaches.

_____

_____

Group 16   1. Another tourist attraction in Bogota is shopping for Colombia's famous emeralds.
2. The underground Salt Cathedral is an interesting side trip for the Bogota visitor.

_____

_____

Group 17   1. Its many rivers and coastal waters make Uruguay famous for its fishing.
2. Boating is also a famous Uruguayan sport.

_____

_____

Group 18   1. The visitor to Montevideo, the capital of Uruguay, can enjoy visiting the many beautiful rose gardens in the daytime.
2. He can also enjoy seeing an excellent theatrical production in the evening.

_____

_____

_____

Group 19   1. A new experience for the Uruguayan tourist is drinking *Yerba maté*, a Latin American tea.
2. Another new experience is eating *asado con cuero*, a steer cooked in its hide.

_____

_____

_____

1. Understanding the needs of Third World nations is often the result of a visit to South America.

2. A visit to South America can also result in an appreciation of the contributions of Latin American artists.

Group 20

_____

_____

Write five original sentences containing compound gerunds or compound gerund phrases.

1. _____

_____

_____

2. _____

_____

_____

3. _____

_____

_____

4. _____

_____

_____

5. _____

_____

_____

EXERCISE 2
Compound Gerunds and Gerund Phrases

Each of the following groups of sentences is to be combined into one sentence containing a compound gerund or gerund phrase. In order to do this, it may be necessary in some instances to completely rephrase one or both of the sentences.

1. Early settlers came to North America in hopes of gaining religious freedom.

2. They also wanted to achieve economic security.

Group 1

_____

_____

1. Some Europeans came to the New World for the purpose of finding gold.

2. Still others wanted to spread Christianity.

Group 2

_____

_____

Group 3
1. Some colonists learned to grow corn from the Indians.
2. They also learned from the Indians how to make clothes from animal skins.

_____

_____

Group 4
1. Colonial women had the responsibility of spinning thread from cotton and wool.
2. They also had to weave the thread into cloth.

_____

_____

Group 5
1. Colonial men had the responsibility of protecting the settlements from the Indians.
2. They also had to provide food and shelter for their families.

_____

_____

Group 6
1. Hunting wild game was a necessity rather than a leisure-time sport for the American colonists.
2. Fishing was not a sport but a means of providing much-needed food.

_____

_____

Group 7
1. In New England playing cards was against the law.
2. The New Englanders were also forbidden to drink alcoholic beverages.

_____

_____

Group 8
1. One of the most popular summer sports in New York was bowling.
2. A popular New York winter sport was ice skating.

_____

_____

Group 9
1. In the southern colonies, horse racing was a popular pastime.
2. Cock fighting was also popular in the South.

_____

_____

Group 10
1. To travel, the American colonists depended on riding horses.
2. The colonists also rowed canoes and rafts to get from one place to another.

_____

_____

1. Cleaning house on Sunday was forbidden by law in Puritan New England.
2. Preparing food on Sunday was also unlawful in Puritan communities.

Group 11

_____

_____

1. In the northern colonies the farmers and their families did their own planting.
2. They also harvested their crops.

Group 12

_____

_____

1. The plantation owners in the South spent their time in planning their crops.
2. They then issued orders for the implementation of their plans.

Group 13

_____

_____

1. Many New Englanders made a profitable living by fishing.
2. Others engaged in whaling, another lucrative occupation.

Group 14

_____

_____

1. For their livelihood the Southerners depended primarily on growing cotton and tobacco for the export market.
2. They also raised herds of cattle and sheep for the domestic market.

Group 15

_____

_____

_____

1. Eventually, distilling rum became an important colonial industry.
2. In time, milling flour also became an important colonial industry.

Group 16

_____

_____

1. Fighting fires was the responsibility of all adult male citizens of the colonial community.
2. They also had to police the streets.

Group 17

_____

_____

1. Punishment for breaking the laws included wearing an iron collar and standing in a pillory.

Group 18

2. More severe punishment included branding with a hot iron and hanging in the town square.

_____

_____

Group 19   **1.** Sewing was an important part of the education of young girls in the American colonies.

                2. It was also important that they learned to embroider.

_____

_____

Group 20   **1.** Studying the culture of colonial America can be interesting as well as enjoyable.

                2. It is also interesting and enjoyable to learn more about our American heritage.

_____

_____

Write five original sentences containing a compound gerund or a compound gerund phrase.

1. _____

_____

_____

2. _____

_____

_____

3. _____

_____

_____

4. _____

_____

_____

5. _____

_____

_____

Compound Infinitive Phrases

THIS lesson is designed to familiarize you with infinitive phrases and to show how the use of such phrases can improve sentence structure and thus improve your writing.

By definition, an infinitive is the word *to* plus a verb. For example, *to sing, to walk, to vote, to study,* and *to drive* are infinitives. An infinitive phrase is an infinitive plus its object and modifiers. For example, *to have breakfast at Sardi's* is an infinitive phrase made up of the infinitive *to have,* plus the object *breakfast,* plus *at Sardi's,* a prepositional phrase functioning as an adverb. Infinitives and infinitive phrases can be used as nouns, as adjectives, or as adverbs in a sentence. For example, in the sentence

Jane and her sister like to play tennis.

to play tennis is an infinitive phrase made up of the word *to* plus the verb *play* plus the object *tennis.* The phrase functions as a noun, for it is the direct object of the verb *like;* that is, it answers the question "What do Jane and her sister like?"

Furthermore, in the sentence

To ignore children is unpardonable.

to ignore children is an infinitive phrase made up of the word *to,* plus the verb *ignore,* plus the object *children.* The phrase functions as a noun because it is the subject of the verb *is.*

Infinitives and infinitive phrases can also function as adjectives; that is, they can describe, limit, or point out by answering the questions "What kind?" "How many?" or "Which one?" For example, in the sentence

The girl to see is Ann.

the infinitive *to see* functions as an adjective answering the question "Which girl?"

Furthermore, infinitives and infinitive phrases can also be used as adverbs. For example, in the sentence

George played to win.

the infinitive *to win* answers the question "How did George play?" Therefore, the infinitive is used as an adverb modifying *played*.

It is often possible to combine two sentences, each of which contains an infinitive or an infinitive phrase functioning as the same part of speech, into one sentence containing a compound infinitive or a compound infinitive phrase. For example, the two sentences

The Spaniards came to America to find gold.
They also wanted to Christianize the Indians.

can be combined by writing one sentence containing a compound infinitive phrase.

The Spaniards came to America to find gold and to Christianize the Indians.

By thus combining the two sentences, superfluous words can be eliminated, and thus writing is improved.

EXERCISE 1
Compound Infinitive Phrases

Each of the following groups of sentences is to be combined into one sentence containing a compound infinitive or a compound infinitive phrase. When you have completed the exercise, refer to the section entitled "Suggested Answers" and examine one of the possible ways that each sentence group can be combined into one sentence by using an infinitive or an infinitive phrase.

Group 1
1. The O'Toole family planned to go to Ireland to visit their ancestral home.
2. Another reason that the O'Toole family wanted to go to Ireland was to become acquainted with relatives whom they had never seen.

_____

_____

Group 2
1. After much discussion, the O'Tooles decided to fly to Dublin.

2. They also decided to stay at a small family hotel in the center of the city.

_____

_____

1. This type of lodging would enable them to meet Irish natives rather than other American tourists.

2. Staying at a small Irish hotel would also make it easier for them to talk with the natives of Ireland.

_____

_____

Group 3

1. A central location in Dublin would make it possible for them to walk to many places of interest.

2. Walking would save them money in transportation fees.

_____

_____

Group 4

1. On the evening of their arrival, the O'Tooles arranged to have dinner in their rooms.

2. They then retired early.

_____

_____

Group 5

1. Before retiring, however, Mr. O'Toole called the manager to compliment the food.

2. He asked the manager to awaken him at six the following morning.

_____

_____

Group 6

1. The next day the four O'Tooles decided to go their separate ways.

2. They planned to meet at the hotel for dinner at six in the evening.

_____

_____

Group 7

1. Mr. O'Toole intended to visit the Census Bureau.

2. His visit was for the purpose of examining the O'Toole family records.

_____

_____

Group 8

1. Mrs. O'Toole wanted to shop in the stores along O'Connell Street.

Group 9

2. She intended to buy souvenirs for her friends at home.

_____

_____

Group 10   **1.** Katie O'Toole planned to telephone an old college friend.
              2. She wanted to invite her friend to lunch.

_____

_____

Group 11   **1.** Peter O'Toole decided to visit the University of Dublin.
              2. He was interested in examining the records concerning the Easter Rebellion.

_____

_____

Group 12   **1.** Peter's research would enable him to collect the missing data he needed.
              2. He could then complete his article for the *Journal of Irish History*.

_____

_____

Group 13   **1.** Mr. O'Toole wanted to find the address of his second cousin, Michael O'Toole.
              2. He also hoped to discover the names of other O'Toole relatives.

_____

_____

Group 14   **1.** Mr. O'Toole's lifelong desire to find his cousin was successful.
              2. His determination to learn the names of other living relatives led to a family reunion within the week.

_____

_____

Group 15   **1.** After the reunion the O'Toole family left Dublin to visit their ancestral home in Cork County.
              2. They also went to the Castle of Blarney, where they kissed the Blarney Stone.

_____

_____

Group 16   **1.** According to legend, a person who kisses the Blarney Stone acquires the power to speak eloquently.

2. He is also able to persuade his listeners to do as he would
have them do.

_____

_____

1. After leaving Cork County, the O'Tooles toured the countryside to see the ruins of ancient ivy-covered monasteries.
2. They also enjoyed the Lakes of Killarney and other magnificent Irish scenery.

_____

_____

Group 17

1. Finally the O'Tooles visited the west coast of Ireland to hike
along the coastal cliffs.
2. They also enjoyed the wide expanse of lonely beaches.

_____

_____

Group 18

1. At the last minute the O'Tooles decided to return to Dublin.
2. From Dublin they would fly back to the United States.

_____

_____

Group 19

1. For many years the O'Toole family would be able to remember with pleasure their visit to Ireland.
2. They would know that family ties to the old country were
not yet broken.

_____

_____

_____

Group 20

Write five original sentences containing compound infinitives or infinitive phrases.

1. _____

_____

_____

2. _____

_____

_____

3. _____

_____

_____

4. _____

_____

_____

5. _____

_____

_____

_____

EXERCISE 2
Compound Infinitive Phrases

Each of the following groups of sentences is to be combined into one sentence containing a compound infinitive phrase.

Group 1
1. Many Englishmen came to the New World to free themselves from religious persecution.
2. Other Englishmen came to America to find new sources of wealth.

_____

_____

Group 2
1. Many early settlers were unable to endure the hardships they encountered in the New World.
2. Others found that they were unable to live peacefully with the Indians.

_____

_____

Group 3
1. Consequently, some early settlers decided to give up their newly found freedom.
2. These settlers returned to England.

_____

_____

Group 4
1. There were others, however, who decided to stay.
2. These people were determined to make a success of their new life through hard work and sacrifice.

_____

_____

Group 5
1. Among those who stayed were the Puritans in Massachusetts, who were eager to maintain their religious freedom.
2. These Puritans also wanted to enjoy a democratic form of government.

_____

_____

Group 6
1. After several years of privation, the settlers in Virginia began to establish large plantations.

2. They began to grow and export large quantities of cotton and tobacco.

_____

_____

1. Colonists under the leadership of Lord Baltimore settled in Maryland in order to worship in the Catholic Church.
2. These colonists wanted to rear their children in the Catholic tradition.

Group 7

_____

_____

1. James Oglethorpe's purpose in founding a colony in Georgia was to help free some of the unfortunate debtors confined to English prisons.
2. Oglethorpe's colony also served as a defense outpost against the Spaniards and the Indians.

Group 8

_____

_____

1. For many years the Dutch did not want to establish permanent settlements in the New World.
2. They preferred to make money by trading with the Indians for furs.

Group 9

_____

_____

1. Eventually, Dutch farmers were persuaded to settle in the New World after the trading companies promised to transport them across the Atlantic free of charge.
2. They were also promised the use of farms and livestock.
3. Ownership of these farms, they were told, could easily be theirs within five years.

Group 10

_____

_____

_____

1. William Penn established a colony where the Quakers would be allowed to worship as they pleased.
2. They were also allowed to live simple lives in a democratic community.

Group 11

_____

_____

1. French explorers came to what is now Canada to search for wealth and power.

Group 12

2. Other Frenchmen wanted to discover a northwest water route to the Far East.

_____

_____

Group 13

1. Catholic priests came to the French settlements in Canada in order to Christianize the Indians.
2. These priests also wanted to extend the power of the Catholic Church in the New World.

_____

_____

Group 14

1. La Salle came to the New World from France to establish trading posts along the St. Lawrence River and the Great Lakes.
2. He also dreamed of building a French fort at the mouth of the Mississippi River.

_____

_____

Group 15

1. La Salle's exploration gave France the opportunity to claim all the land drained by the Mississippi River and its tributaries.
2. His explorations also gave France the opportunity to build settlements and forts in this territory.

_____

_____

_____

Group 16

1. Franciscan priests came from Spain to what is now the southwestern part of the United States to Christianize the Indians.
2. They also wanted to make the Indians an industrious and productive people.

_____

_____

Group 17

1. Eventually these Indians, under the direction of the priests, were able to put many acres of land into cultivation.
2. They also managed to build up a small but lucrative trade with other countries.

_____

_____

Group 18

1. The English in America were the first Europeans to become dissatisfied with their role as colonists.

2. They were the first to declare their independence from the mother country.

_____

_____

Group 19

1. Under the able leadership of such men as Samuel Adams and George Washington, the English in America were able to free themselves of foreign domination.
2. They established a new and independent nation.

_____

_____

Group 20

1. Eventually the new nation managed to purchase vast areas from the French and the Spanish.
2. They also managed to claim additional territory by right of occupation.
3. They thus extended the borders from the Atlantic to the Pacific and from Canada to Mexico.

_____

_____

_____

Write five original sentences containing compound infinitive phrases.

1. _____

_____

_____

2. _____

_____

_____

3. _____

_____

_____

4. _____

_____

_____

5. _____

_____

_____

Combining Sentences by Using Adjective Clauses

THIS exercise provides practice in combining sentences by using adjective clauses. In Lesson 6 you were given an explanation of the word *adjective* and told how an adjective functions in a sentence. It was explained that an adjective answers the questions "How many?" "Which one?" and "What kind?" Thus an adjective numbers, points out, and describes. A clause that numbers, points out, or describes is referred to as an adjective clause. By definition a clause is a group of words with a subject and a predicate verb. If this group of words expresses a complete thought, it is called an independent clause. If, however, this group of words does not express a complete thought, it is called a dependent clause because it depends on the remainder of the sentence for complete sense. In this lesson we are concerned with dependent clauses used as adjectives; that is, those that point out, number, or describe. These adjective clauses usually begin with the relative pronouns *who, whom, whose, which,* and *that.*

If we examine the sentence

> The assistant professor who recently published the book entitled *Caravan to Africa* has been promoted to associate professor.

we discover that there is a group of words beginning with the relative pronoun *who* and containing the subject *who* and the predicate verb *published.* The group of words

> who recently published the book entitled *Caravan to Africa*

answers the question "Which assistant professor has been promoted to associate professor?" It is thus an adjective clause that points out.

In the sentence

Acadiana University, which is a small liberal arts school, is located in southwest Louisiana.

the group of words

which is a small liberal arts school

begins with the relative pronoun *which,* contains the subject *which* and the predicate verb *is,* and tells what kind of school Acadiana University is. It is thus an adjective clause that describes.

It is often possible to combine two sentences into one by converting one of the sentences into an adjective clause. Thus by writing one sentence rather than two, you can tighten your sentence structure and, at the same time, achieve sentence variety. For example, the two sentences

The Metropolitan Museum contains some of the world's most priceless paintings.
This museum is located in New York City.

can be combined by using an adjective clause and writing

The Metropolitan Museum, which contains some of the world's most priceless paintings, is located in New York City.

Furthermore, the two sentences

George overuses a transitional word in his essays.
This word is *consequently.*

can be combined by using an adjective clause that points out; that is, it answers the question "Which one?"

The transitional word that George overuses in his essays is *consequently.*

Combining Sentences by Using Adjective Clauses

In this exercise you are to combine the sentences in each group into one sentence by using an adjective clause. When you have completed the exercise, refer to the section entitled "Suggested Answers" and examine one of the possible ways each group of sentences can be combined into one sentence containing an adjective clause.

1. Our European tour took us to the Iberian Peninsula.   *Group 1*
2. The Iberian Peninsula includes the countries of Spain and Portugal.

_____

_____

Group 2

1. In Portugal we visited the capital city of Lisbon.
2. Lisbon is located on the right bank of the Tagus River.

_____

_____

Group 3

1. An interesting Spanish city on our tour was serene and color-ful Seville.
2. Seville lies in the center of Spain's wine country.

_____

_____

Group 4

1. In Granada we saw the Alhambra, a centuries-old Moorish castle.
2. The Alhambra is a melange of marble courts, patios, mosaics, and gardens.

_____

_____

Group 5

1. Farther north in Toledo we toured El Greco's museumlike home.
2. Some of the works of this famous Spanish painter are dis-played in this building.

_____

_____

Group 6

1. The Prado Museum contains the world's largest collection of El Greco's paintings.
2. The Prado Museum is located in Madrid.

_____

_____

Group 7

1. The enormous monastery palace of Escorial was built by Philip II.
2. Escorial contains priceless tapestries, works of art, and crypts of Spanish kings.

_____

_____

Group 8

1. The Valley of the Fallen is located near Madrid.
2. The Valley of the Fallen is a moving memorial to those who died in the Spanish Civil War.

_____

_____

Group 9

1. Northwest of Madrid the tourist can visit picturesque Palen-cia.

2. Palencia is the site of Spain's oldest university.

_____

_____

1. Santiago de Compostela is an ancient Spanish town.   *Group 10*
2. It is located in northwestern Spain.
3. Santiago de Compostela was a center for pilgrimages for hundreds of years.

_____

_____

_____

1. A beautiful eleventh-century cathedral is also located in Santiago de Compostela.   *Group 11*
2. This cathedral is said to be the spiritual resting place of St. James the Apostle.

_____

_____

1. From Spain we went to Italy.   *Group 12*
2. Italy is a boot-shaped peninsula jutting into the Mediterranean Sea.

_____

_____

1. Our first stop in Italy was Rome.   *Group 13*
2. Rome is an ancient yet modern city.
3. This city is located on the Tiber River.

_____

_____

_____

1. Rome is probably the most historically significant city in Europe.   *Group 14*
2. In Rome one can visit, among other famous landmarks, the Vatican, the Pantheon, the Appian Way, and the Sistine Chapel.

_____

_____

_____

1. The Vatican stands on the *Vaticanus Mons,* or Vatican Hill.   *Group 15*
2. The *Vaticanus Mons* got its name because it was the meeting place of the ancient *vaticinatores,* or soothsayers.

_____

_____

Group 16
1. The Pantheon was built by Agrippa, son-in-law of Augustus, who was the Roman emperor from 27 B.C. to 17 A.D.
2. The Pantheon has been used as a Christian church since the seventh century.

_____

_____

Group 17
1. The Appian Way goes from Rome to Brindisi by way of Capua.
2. The Appian Way, begun in the fourth century B.C., is the oldest and best of all the Roman roads.

_____

_____

Group 18
1. The Sistine Chapel was built in 1473.
2. The ceiling of the Sistine Chapel is decorated with the famous frescoes painted by Michelangelo.

_____

_____

Group 19
1. North of Rome on the Arno River lies the beautiful city of Florence.
2. Florence has often been called the storehouse of the world's art treasures.

_____

_____

Group 20
1. Still farther north in spectacular Venice one can visit the famous Bridge of Sighs.
2. The Bridge of Sighs connects the palace of the doge with the state prisons.
3. On this bridge, prisoners were once escorted from the courtroom to the scaffold.

_____

_____

_____

_____

When you have finished this exercise, write five original sentences each of which contains an adjective clause.

1. _____

_____

_____

2. _____

_____

_____

3. _____
_____
_____

4. _____
_____
_____

5. _____
_____
_____

Combining Sentences by Using Adjective Clauses

Again in this exercise you are to combine the sentences in each group by using an adjective clause.

1. Fennec foxes have rather large ears in proportion to their overall size.
2. These little foxes occupy desert regions.

Group 1

_____
_____

1. Kangaroo rats can live without drinking water.
2. These desert rats grow to about a foot in length.

Group 2

_____
_____

1. Another desert animal is the chuckwalla, a member of the lizard family.
2. This harmless animal is native to the desert regions of the southwestern part of the United States.

Group 3

_____
_____

1. The skink is also a member of the lizard family.
2. Many skinks have no legs.
3. Skinks are desert animals.

Group 4

_____
_____
_____

1. Gila monsters are lizards native to the desert regions of the United States and Mexico.

Group 5

2. These are the only North American lizards with a poisonous bite.

_____

_____

Group 6 **1.** The horned toad is a harmless North American lizard.
2. This small desert animal is an insectivore; that is, it eats insects rather than plants.

_____

_____

Group 7 **1.** Another desert animal found in the United States is the prairie dog.
2. These rodents live in underground burrows.

_____

_____

Group 8 **1.** The sidewinder, or horned rattlesnake, is a small desert rattlesnake only two feet long.
2. Like other larger rattlesnakes, the sidewinder's bite is extremely dangerous.

_____

_____

Group 9 **1.** The coyote lives in the deserts and prairies of western North America.
2. The coyote is a carnivore of the dog family; that is, it eats the flesh of other animals.

_____

_____

Group 10 **1.** The study of birds has long been a fascinating hobby for many people.
2. Such a study often results in increased knowledge concerning kinds of birds, habits of birds, history of birds, and importance of birds.

_____

_____

Group 11 **1.** One group of birds cannot fly.
2. This group includes the kiwi, the cassowary, and the rhea.

_____

_____

1. The kiwi is a flightless bird native to New Zealand.
2. The kiwi is a nocturnal bird; that is, it is active only at night.

Group 12

_____

_____

1. The cassowary is native to Australia.
2. It can not only run rapidly but also jump high.

Group 13

_____

_____

1. The rhea is a flightless bird.
2. It can be found in South America.
3. It looks like a small ostrich.

Group 14

_____

_____

_____

1. The red hornbill can be found in India.
2. It is one of the strangest looking of all birds, with its curved yellow and red beak; long, crooked neck; awkward-looking black wings; and thin, white tail feathers.

Group 15

_____

_____

1. The largest known bird is the male ostrich of Africa.
2. It often achieves a weight of over 300 pounds.
3. The smallest known bird is the bee hummingbird of Cuba.
4. It weighs about one and a half ounces.

Group 16

_____

_____

_____

_____

1. A few years ago the whooping crane was rapidly becoming extinct.
2. It is now protected in national bird sanctuaries.

Group 17

_____

_____

1. Wild ducks and geese are protected by game laws.
2. These laws limit the number of birds that can be shot.
3. These laws also determine the time of the year they can be shot.

Group 18

_____

_____

_____

LESSON 11: COMBINING SENTENCES BY USING ADJECTIVE CLAUSES / 115

When you have finished this exercise, write five original sentences, each of which contains at least one adjective clause.

1. _____
   _____
   _____

2. _____
   _____
   _____

3. _____
   _____
   _____

4. _____
   _____
   _____

5. _____
   _____
   _____

Combining Sentences by Using Adverbial Clauses

THIS exercise provides practice in combining sentences by using adverbial clauses. In Lesson 7 you were given an explanation of the word *adverb* and told how an adverb functions in a sentence. It was explained that an adverb answers the questions "How?" "When?" "Where?" and "For what reason?" and thus indicates manner, time, place, and cause. A clause—that is, a group of words with a subject and predicate—that indicates manner, time, place, and cause is called an adverbial clause. These clauses, which answer the questions "How?" "When?" "Where?" and "For what reason?" begin with such words as

because
as soon as
before
after
although
as if
if
until

Such clauses do not express a complete thought and therefore are called dependent clauses. These clauses are called dependent clauses because they depend on the rest of the sentence for complete sense. If we examine the sentence

After the farmer killed the steer, he skinned and dressed it, cut it up into steaks and roasts, and put it in his freezer.

The words *after the farmer killed the steer* answer the question "When did the farmer skin and dress the steer, cut it up, and put it in his freezer?" It is therefore a dependent clause containing the subject *farmer* and the predicate verb *killed,* which indicates time by answering the question "When?"

In the sentence

Because not much snow had fallen in Vail, the ski enthusiasts had to postpone their vacations.

because not much snow had fallen in Vail is a group of words with the subject *snow* and the predicate verb *had fallen,* which answers the question "For what reason did the ski enthusiasts have to postpone their vacation?" It thus indicates cause and is, therefore, an adverbial clause.

In this exercise you are to combine the two sentences in each group by converting one sentence into an adverbial clause using such words as *when, as soon as, although, until,* and *after* and adding it to the other sentence. For example, the two sentences

We landed in Paris at midnight.
We then drove to our hotel.

can be combined by adding *after* to the first sentence and joining it to the second sentence, thus:

After we landed in Paris at midnight, we drove to our hotel.

Similarly, the two sentences

We checked into the hotel.
We were promptly escorted to our room.

can be combined by adding *as soon as* to the first sentence and combining it with the second sentence, thus:

As soon as we checked into the hotel, we were promptly escorted to our room.

EXERCISE 1
Combining Sentences by Using Adverbial Clauses

In this exercise you are to combine the sentences in each group into one sentence that contains an adverbial clause. Again, when you have finished, refer to the section entitled "Suggested Answers" and examine one of the possible ways that each sentence group can be combined into one sentence containing an adverbial clause.

Group 1
1. We bought our tickets and checked our bags at Kennedy International Airport.

2. We then boarded a Pan American jetliner bound for South America.

_____

_____

1. We could have toured the major cities of South America such as Rio de Janeiro and Buenos Aires.

2. We decided, however, to see such out-of-the way places as Iguassu Falls and the Galapagos Islands.

_____

_____

Group 2

1. Torrential rains greeted us at Lake Titicaca.

2. We were unable to enjoy the hydrofoil boat ride across the lake.

_____

_____

Group 3

1. We arrived in Montevideo at noon.

2. Not until our arrival did we discover that a gaucho barbecue had been arranged for us at Faraut's Winery.

_____

_____

Group 4

1. Many small South American farmers are unacquainted with modern farm equipment and methods.

2. Yields on many small South American farms are extremely poor.

_____

_____

Group 5

1. The piranha is a flesh-eating fish found in many South American rivers.

2. Swimming in these rivers is, therefore, a dangerous pastime.

_____

_____

Group 6

1. The South American section of the Pan American Highway was completed in the 1960s.

2. It was then possible to travel from Ecuador to Argentina by car.

_____

_____

Group 7

1. An automobile trip across South America is not always comfortable.

Group 8

2. Some sections of the highway are rough and dusty in dry weather and muddy and treacherous in wet weather.

_____

_____

Group 9

1. Ornithologists, or those who study birds, like to visit South America.
2. Exotic birds such as egrets, toucans, flamingos, and parrots are found in large numbers in South America.

_____

_____

Group 10

1. A tourist can spend two days traveling on a local train from Guayaquil to Quito, a distance of about three hundred miles.
2. This trip affords a look at lush tropical plantations; breathtaking mountain scenery; swirling river currents; and quiet, secluded lakes.

_____

_____

Group 11

1. Venezuela is blessed with many miles of excellent highways.
2. The best way to see Venezuela is by car.

_____

_____

Group 12

1. Many people who work in Caracas live in beautiful homes and apartments along the coast.
2. Superhighways have made the adjoining coastal area easily accessible to Caracas.

_____

_____

Group 13

1. Caracas is located in a valley about 3,000 feet above sea level.
2. Its location and elevation result in mild temperatures throughout the year.

_____

_____

Group 14

1. The Venezuelan *llanos*, or plains, which lie between the mountains and the Orinoco River, are a hunter's paradise.
2. Many wild animals and exotic birds live here.

_____

_____

Group 15

1. We left Venezuela in early May.

2. We then flew to Paraguay, a small country lying between Brazil and Argentina.

_____

_____

1. Visitors to small Paraguayan villages are impressed by the clean adobe houses and the neat village squares.
2. These villages, however, have no modern conveniences such as electricity, running water, and sewage systems.

Group 16

_____

_____

1. We spent a week seeing as much of the Paraguayan country-side as possible.
2. We then left for Uruguay.

Group 17

_____

_____

1. Uruguay is the smallest republic in South America.
2. Uruguayans enjoy the highest standard of living in South America as a result of vast reforms, which broke up large plantations and gave the land to the people.

Group 18

_____

_____

1. We drove for several hours through the streets of Monte-video, the capital of Uruguay.
2. We were impressed with the many parks filled with beautiful trees and colorful flowers.

Group 19

_____

_____

1. We did not have time to visit the Island of the Lions, which is famous for its seals and sea lions.
2. We did have a good view of the island as we left Montevideo by plane for home.

Group 20

_____

_____

_____

When you have completed this exercise, write five original sentences containing adverbial clauses.

1. _____

_____

_____

2. _____
_____
_____
_____

3. _____
_____
_____
_____

4. _____
_____
_____

5. _____
_____
_____
_____

EXERCISE 2
Combining Sentences by Using Adverbial Clauses

In this exercise you are again to combine the sentences in each group into one sentence containing an adverbial clause.

Group 1
1. Greenland is a huge glacial island.
2. Crops, however, are grown along the coast, which is green and fertile.

_____
_____

Group 2
1. During most of the year, temperatures are extremely low in Greenland.
2. The summers, however, are extremely hot.

_____
_____

Group 3
1. Greenland is strategically located between Europe, North America, and the Orient.
2. The Sondre Strom Airport in Greenland has become an important stopover for transpolar commercial airplanes.

_____
_____

Group 4
1. Enemy occupation of Greenland would be militarily disastrous for the United States.
2. The United States Air Force has a large military installation at Thule in northern Greenland.

_____
_____

1. Glaciers fall from the land and drop into the sea.
2. The glaciers then become floating icebergs, a constant menace to ships crossing the northern part of the Atlantic Ocean.

Group 5

_____

_____

_____

1. For several decades the waters off the western coast of Greenland have become significantly warmer.
2. More and more natives became fishermen.

Group 6

_____

_____

_____

1. Greenland can be seen from some high peaks in Iceland.
2. The island was unoccupied until the tenth century.

Group 7

_____

_____

1. The first colony in Greenland survived for five centuries.
2. It suddenly and mysteriously disappeared.

Group 8

_____

_____

1. Greenland is rich in gold and silver deposits.
2. Miners have had little success in removing the minerals from the earth.

Group 9

_____

_____

1. Greenland is not popular with tourists.
2. Luxurious accommodations for visitors are practically nonexistent.

Group 10

_____

_____

1. The interior regions of Iceland are largely uninhabitable.
2. Most Icelanders live along the coast.

Group 11

_____

_____

1. Water from Iceland's hot springs was not piped into the city of Reykjavik until 1930.
2. The water from these springs now heats the city.

Group 12

_____

_____

Group 13
1. Water from Iceland's many waterfalls is harnassed by huge hydroelectric plants.
2. Electricity is therefore cheap.

_____

_____

Group 14
1. Iceland is strategically located.
2. British and American troops occupied the island during World War II.

_____

_____

Group 15
1. Tourism is not encouraged in Iceland.
2. Visitors are given a warm and cordial welcome.

_____

_____

Group 16
1. Laki, a volcano in southern Iceland, erupted in the late eighteenth century.
2. More than half of Iceland's livestock was destroyed.

_____

_____

Group 17
1. Many greenhouses heated by the hot-water springs have recently been built in Iceland.
2. Vegetables can now be grown in abundance.

_____

_____

Group 18
1. Iceland recently extended the fishing limits from four to twelve miles off the coast.
2. Many disputes with other countries resulted from this extension.

_____

_____

_____

Group 19
1. The disputes over fishing limits were eventually settled.
2. Now fishermen from Iceland and other nations fish together peacefully.

_____

_____

Group 20
1. For many years Iceland's economy depended primarily on the fur industry.

2. Today the economy of Iceland depends largely on the fishing industry.

_____

_____

Now write five original sentences containing adverbial clauses.

1. _____

_____

_____

2. _____

_____

_____

3. _____

_____

_____

4. _____

_____

_____

5. _____

_____

_____

Paragraph Construction: The Basic Elements

A good expository paragraph consists of a group of sentences aimed at explaining a single idea. Since most of the writing that you as a student will be called on to do is expository, it is important for you to learn how to construct an expository paragraph. First, you should learn how to construct a good topic sentence; that is, you ought to learn how to write a sentence that announces to the reader the central idea of the paragraph. Next, you should consider the basic elements of a good paragraph. These elements are unity, coherence, and emphasis. Finally, you should learn how to develop the central idea by such methods as example, definition, comparison and contrast, cause and effect, and classification or division or by a combination of these methods.

A good expository paragraph contains a topic sentence. Such a sentence not only announces the topic of the paragraph but also makes a definitive statement about that topic. Thus the topic sentence can be defined as a sentence that contains the central idea to be discussed in a single paragraph. Although this sentence can be placed at the beginning, in the middle, or at the end of a paragraph, you would do well to place it at the beginning so that you as well as your reader will have the controlling idea clearly in mind from the outset.

After you have formulated the topic sentence, you should make certain that every subsequent sentence contains information that supports the idea presented in the topic sentence. By doing this you will achieve unity; that is, you will eliminate all information that is not pertinent to the main idea. Unity, however, is only one of the three basic elements of a good paragraph. The other two are coherence and emphasis. Coherence is achieved by using words and phrases that link the sentences together to make them cohere or stick together so that there is no break in the pattern of thought. Finally, a good paragraph will have emphasis; that is, the information presented will go from the least to the most important.

In order to understand the nature of a topic sentence, examine the following statement:

> It is becoming increasingly apparent that regular and prolonged use of marijuana can have adverse effects on the smoker.

It is apparent that the topic of the sentence is marijuana, but it is also apparent that a definitive statement is made about marijuana. That statement defines or announces the specific aspects of the topic that will be discussed in the paragraph, aspects such as regular and prolonged use and the adverse effects of such use. Consequently, the writer would not discuss such ideas as the method of growing marijuana, the illegal importation of marijuana, the penalties involved in the possession of marijuana, or the increased use of marijuana among young teenagers. On the other hand, he would limit himself to a discussion of the bad effects of regular and prolonged use of the drug and would write a paragraph somewhat like the following:

> It is becoming increasingly apparent that regular and prolonged use of marijuana can have adverse effects on the smoker. Many psychologists agree that over a period of time, consistent smoking of marijuana causes unfavorable personality changes in the user. These psychologists also agree that such use often destroys the ambition and drive of the smoker. Furthermore, physicians are beginning to observe increasing sterility among those who frequently smoke the weed. But even more important, research scientists have discovered that the incidence of lung cancer among smokers of marijuana is about sixteen times greater than among smokers of tobacco. These effects, which were not so apparent a decade ago, may be only the first in a longer list of dangerous side effects resulting from consistent, long-term use of marijuana.

The supporting sentences in this paragraph discuss *effects* and nothing more. Thus the writer has achieved unity. He has also used such transitional words and phrases as *consistent use, furthermore,* and *but even more important*. The use of such transitions makes the various sentences cohere or stick together so that the ideas flow smoothly along with no abrupt break in thought. The writer thus achieves coherence, another basic element of a good paragraph. Finally, the writer begins with what appears to be the least dangerous effect of the regular and prolonged use of marijuana, unfavorable personality changes, and proceeds to the most dangerous, lung cancer. In this way he achieves emphasis, the third basic element of a good paragraph.

EXERCISE 1
Paragraph Construction: The Basic Elements

In the following exercise, you are to read carefully the sentences containing the supporting information in each paragraph and then supply a topic sentence for that paragraph. It is important that the topic sentence be a clear, definitive statement of the central idea of the paragraph.

1. _____
   _____
   _____
   _____
   _____

Some students attend college to enjoy the social life that a university campus offers. Others go to college because their parents expect them to. Still others go because their best friends are going. There are also a few students who attend college because they do not want to find jobs and support themselves. However, there seems to be an increasing number of students who attend college to become better educated and better prepared for a meaningful career.

2. _____
   _____
   _____
   _____
   _____

In Spain the king's personal guard is wounded and three people are killed when two men throw a bomb at an army staff car. In San Salvador three American nuns are brutally murdered by unknown assailants. In Washington, D.C., President Ronald Reagan, along with his press secretary and two bodyguards, narrowly escapes death when an assassin opens fire in an attempt to kill the chief executive of the United States. In the Vatican City Pope John Paul II is critically wounded by bullets allegedly fired from the gun of an escaped murderer and suspected KGB associate who had vowed to end the life of the spiritual leader of all Roman

Catholics. These are only a few of the acts of violence and terrorism that have shocked the world in less than a year.

3. _____
_____
_____
_____
_____

There is a large contingent of students on the campus who are natives of Venezuela. Most of these students are majoring in either agriculture or petroleum engineering. Another large group of students attending the University of Southwestern Louisiana include the Iranians, who are primarily interested in such fields as geology and petroleum engineering. The third significant group of students from other countries at U.S.L. is made up of Nigerians, whose majors range from nursing to computer science. Venezuelans, Iranians, Nigerians, as well as a sprinkling of East Indians, Australians, and Filipinos give the U.S.L. campus an international aura.

4. _____
_____
_____
_____
_____

The fifty-five-mile-an-hour speed limit on the nation's highways has significantly reduced the consumption of gasoline in the United States and thus has decreased the country's reliance on foreign oil. Furthermore, the number of accidents on the highways has declined since the imposition of the new speed limit. But most important, the number of fatalities and permanent injuries has been significantly lowered since it became unlawful to drive a car over fifty-five miles an hour.

5. _____
_____
_____
_____
_____

Freshwater and deepsea fishing are available for the dedicated angler. Louisiana also offers the hunter such in-season game as ducks, geese, squirrel, and deer. Furthermore, the spectator sportsman can enjoy quarter-horse and thorough-bred racing at racetracks scattered throughout south Louisiana, basketball and football games at the Superdome in New Orleans, and speedboat racing on the many large lakes in the state.

6. _____
   _____
   _____
   _____
   _____

The bank offers a regular savings account that pays 5 percent interest, compounded daily and paid quarterly. No minimum deposit is required. There is also the super savings account, paying 5.75 percent interest for those who make an initial deposit of at least $500 and add to it in amounts of not less than $100. The interest on these accounts is also compounded daily and paid quarterly. For those who have at least $1,000 to invest, the bank offers a time certificate with an interest of 12.5 percent. These certificates, however, must be held for 32 months before they can be redeemed without penalty. Finally, if the investor has at least $10,000, he can purchase a money-market certificate redeemable in 6 months and offering interest based on the prevailing prime rate of interest, which may vary from 10 to 17 percent.

After you have completed the exercise, turn to the section entitled "Answer Section" and examine the topic sentences that could be used for each of the paragraphs.

EXERCISE 2
Paragraph Construction: The Basic Elements

In this exercise you are again to read carefully the supporting sentences in each paragraph and then write an appropriate topic sentence for that paragraph.

1. _____
   _____
   _____
   _____
   _____

First there is the standard eastern dialect spoken by people living in the New England states and in some sections of New York City. Then there is the standard Southern dialect common to the states that are known as the South, along with the southeastern part of Texas. Finally, there is the standard general American dialect, which prevails in the rest of the United States. These three dialects are spoken by the educated and cultured people of the three geographical areas.

2. _____
_____
_____
_____
_____

The smallest bed is the twin-sized bed, which is 39 inches wide and 76 inches long. Next in size is the double bed, also 76 inches long but 54 inches wide. The two largest beds, both 80 inches long, are the queen-sized bed, which is 60 inches wide, and the king-sized bed, which is 78 inches wide.

3. _____
_____
_____
_____
_____

It is not true that a shark is attracted by blood and that a bleeding swimmer is a more likely target than a nonbleeding one. It is not true that a shark circles a victim before it begins the attack. Nor is it true that the shark's attack is motivated by hunger. Neither is it true that a shark will avidly consume its victim. It is also erroneous to believe that there are more than about twenty-five shark attacks worldwide in a single year and that more than 20 percent of these attacks are fatal.

4. _____
_____
_____
_____
_____

He can tune in to a CBS affiliate and enjoy Charles Kuralt, whose sixty-minute morning program includes the latest in fast-breaking worldwide news as well as what we want to know about sports and the weather. His second choice for early morning viewing is "Good Morning America," held together by the veteran television personality David Hartman and available on most ABC-affiliated stations. Finally, the early-morning television viewer can choose NBC's "Today Show," hosted by Tom Brokaw and Jane Pauley and featuring such regulars as weatherman Willard Scott and art critic Gene Shalit.

5. _____

_____

_____

_____

_____

This tortilla, which can be made of ground-up corn or of flour, can be folded and fried and filled with a mixture of diced meat, lettuce, onions, and tomatoes. Thus it becomes a *taco*. It can be cut into pieces, fried, and then dipped in a spicy cheese sauce and called a *nacho*. When wrapped around a mixture of cooked beans and ground meat, it becomes a *burrito*. When the tortilla is rolled around grated cheese and covered with a tangy tomato sauce, it becomes an *enchilada*. A fried tortilla heaped with refried beans, diced lettuce and tomatoes, grated cheese, and mashed avocado becomes a *chalupa con queso*. Or it can be warmed, spread with butter, rolled, and eaten in the same way that bread is eaten with the rest of a meal.

14

Paragraph Construction: Orderly Development by Example

SEVERAL of the paragraphs in the previous lesson are developed by example or enumeration. That is, the writer has chosen to explain the idea contained in the topic sentence by citing several examples that illustrate that idea. For example, in paragraph 2, Exercise 1, Lesson 13, the central idea is that, internationally, terrorism and violence have increased dramatically over the past few years. The writer develops this idea by citing four examples of such violence and terrorism: (1) the attempted assassination of one of the personal guards of King Juan Carlos in Spain; (2) the senseless murder of three American nuns in San Salvador; (3) the attempted assassination of President Ronald Reagan in Washington, D.C.; and (4) the attempted assassination of Pope John Paul II in Vatican City.

Furthermore, in paragraph 3, Exercise 2, Lesson 13, the writer has given six examples to prove that myths and fallacies regarding sharks and their attacks on human beings do, in fact, exist. These examples are (1) that sharks are attracted by blood, (2) that sharks attack because they are hungry, (3) that sharks circle their victims before they attack, (4) that sharks eat their victims, (5) that there are hundreds of shark attacks each year, and (6) that most of these attacks end in death for the victims.

These two paragraphs, then, are developed by citing several examples to support the central idea contained in the topic sentence. This is indeed a useful and workable method of paragraph development by illustration and example.

There are occasions, however, when you may find that one extended example rather than several briefer examples illustrates more forcefully the point you are making. The following paragraph illustrates this fact.

Although water skiing appears to be a safe and exciting sport, it can be hazardous and maiming. This fact became painfully apparent to me last summer when a group of my friends and I were water skiing on Lake Adams, not far from where I live. My best friend David was a skillful skier with more hours on water skis than any other person in our crowd. As he was being pulled in a wide circle behind a fast-moving motor boat, another boat pulling a skier seemed to appear out of nowhere. Somehow David's legs became entangled in the other skier's tow rope, and before we knew what was happening, David was in the water. When we got to him, we were horrified to see that his right leg was almost completely severed just above the knee. Somehow we applied a tourniquet to stop the flow of blood and rushed David to a nearby hospital. The doctors there had two specialists flown in, who tried to reattach the leg. The attempt was a failure. David lived, but one leg was gone. As he learned to walk on his artificial leg, everyone who knew David became painfully aware that water skiing was not the safe and simple sport it once seemed to be.

The central idea of this paragraph, that *water skiing can be hazardous and maiming* is effectively and forcefully illustrated by writing a detailed account of one incident derived from personal experience that illustrates the hazards involved in the sport. A series of more briefly stated examples would not, in all probability, have the impact that the one more graphic illustration has.

You will have to decide for yourself whether a series of examples or one extended example will better illustrate your central idea. Usually the central idea lends itself to one *or* the other of these methods of illustration.

EXERCISE 1
Paragraph Construction:
Orderly Development by Example

Examine the following topic sentences. Choose one of these sentences and develop it into a paragraph by using a series of brief illustrations or by using one extended example drawn from personal experience. Be sure to determine which of these two methods of exemplification is best suited for the development of the particular topic sentence you choose. If you choose to support your central idea by using a series of examples, be certain that you use at least four and be sure that these examples are fitting and specific. If, on the other hand, you find that one extended example would better illustrate your central idea, be certain that it is sufficiently detailed to have an impact on your reader.

1. My grandfather is a man of great compassion.
2. Television offers educational opportunities for adults.
3. Yard work has become simpler as a result of the invention of labor-saving devices.
4. Many career opportunities are open to students who major in mathematics (or English, or foreign language, or art, or drama, and so on).
5. An innocent bystander is sometimes the victim of an attempted crime.

EXERCISE 2
Paragraph Construction:
Orderly Development by Example

Examine the following topic sentences. Choose one of the sentences and develop the idea it contains into a paragraph by using a series of examples or by using one longer extended example. Again, let the topic sentence itself determine which of these two methods would be more effective.

1. Although it is often tempting to be dishonest, honesty can be satisfying and rewarding.
2. Hobbies can become a valuable source of income.
3. Some television commercials offend the sensibilities of many viewers.
4. Fathers (or mothers) can be counted on in a crisis.
5. A person cannot always believe what he hears.

Paragraph Construction: Orderly Development by Definition

15

WHENEVER we read or hear a word that is strange to us, we are curious about its meaning. Normally, we turn to a dictionary to find a definition of the term. These dictionary definitions are referred to as formal definitions. A good formal definition puts the word being defined into a class and then shows how it is different from other terms in the same class. For example, in the definition

A jockey is a person who rides a horse professionally in a race.

the word *jockey* is put into the class of *people who ride horses.* The term is then shown to be different from other riders of horses in that the jockey rides *professionally in a race* rather than for pleasure, or to round up cattle, or for some other reason.

Again, in the definition

A shank is the part of the leg between the knee and the ankle.

the term being defined, *shank,* is put into the class *part of the leg* and then differentiated from other parts of the leg as being located *between the knee and the ankle.*

Formal definitions have their place in the writing of paragraphs. They can be used to clarify terms used in the paragraph or they can be used as the very foundation of a paragraph.

There are terms, however, that cannot be adequately defined or classified by a formal definition. These terms often require longer and less formal definitions in order to make perfectly clear the writer's concept of a particular word or phrase. This is particularly true of such abstract terms as *despair, hope, honor, respect,* and *faith.* However, concrete terms often require extended, informal definitions in order for the writer to make quite clear his concept of the term. Examine the following statement:

> A bigot is a person who refuses to tolerate any creed, nationality, race, or opinion other than his own.

This is a good definition. The term *bigot* is put in the class *person* and then is shown to be different from others in the class in that he refuses to tolerate any creed, nationality, race, or opinion other than his own. But if the writer is to make perfectly clear his concept of the word *bigot*, he extends his definition and writes a paragraph similar to the following:

> A bigot is a person who refuses to tolerate any creed, nationality, race, or opinion other than his own. If he is a Protestant, he thinks all Catholics are idol-worshipping papists. If he is an Anglo-Saxon, he believes all Mexicans are treacherous, all Italians are deceitful, and all Poles are stupid. If he is white, he thinks all blacks are unemployed welfare recipients who vote in a block. If he is a Democrat, he is convinced that all Republicans are wealthy conservatists intent upon waging war and starving the indigent. A bigot is a person the world could do without.

In order to clarify his concept of a bigot, the writer of this paragraph has extended his definition beyond classification and differentiation so that the reader has a fuller understanding of the writer's concept of a bigot's prejudices. Such extended definitions are frequently useful in expository writing, for they furnish complete explanations of words and phrases used by the writer. Thus the reader is quite certain of the writer's definition of such words and phrases.

A more abstract term such as *frustration* might be defined as the feeling a person has when he is unable to accomplish what he has set out to accomplish. In this definition the word to be defined, *frustration*, is put into the class *feeling* and is shown to be different from other feelings because it results from being unable to do what one wants to do. This definition, however, needs to be expanded if the reader is to have a completely clear idea of what the writer's concept of the word *frustration* really is. The writer might expand his definition by explaining how the feeling manifests itself in various situations. In order to do this, he could write an expanded definition similar to the following:

> Frustration is the feeling a person has when he is unable to accomplish what he has set out to accomplish. When a golfer attempts a five-foot putt and misses, his frustration is obvious when he throws his golf club down, utters an oath, and stalks off the green.

When a student, unable to solve a problem in mathematics, slams his book shut and throws his pencil across the room, he is venting his feeling of frustration. The home gardener whose vegetables dry up and die might express his frustration by angrily pulling up the plants and tossing them into the garbage. Whenever a person makes a serious effort to do something and is thwarted in his attempt, he experiences the feeling known as frustration.

After reading this extended or expanded definition of the word *frustration*, a person understands much better what the writer means by the term.

The ability to write extended or expanded definitions can be extremely helpful to the student who is asked to define terms in such subjects as psychology, sociology, biology, physics, history, and so on. This ability is also helpful after the student completes his college work and goes out into the world of work to earn a living. If he becomes an accountant, he will be called upon to define such terms as *capital gains* or *excess profits tax*. If he goes to work in a bank, he might be called upon to define such terms as *compound interest* or *deferred payment*. If he becomes a teacher, he may be asked to define terms such as *curriculum* or *grade-point average*. Whatever he chooses as his life's work, a person will, at one time or another, be asked to define the terms used in his profession. It is, therefore, important to develop the ability to write extended definitions.

EXERCISE 1
Paragraph Construction:
Orderly Development by Definition

Examine the topic sentences listed below. Choose one of the sentences and, using it as a topic sentence, develop a paragraph by writing an extension of the definition as stated in the topic sentence.

1. A fanatic is a person who is excessively devoted to a cause.
2. An egotist is a person who has an inflated sense of his own importance.
3. Ennui is a feeling of weariness or boredom.
4. A dialect is the form of a language spoken in a particular region or by a particular group of people.
5. A spy is a person who secretly observes the actions of others.

Paragraph Construction:
Orderly Development by Definition

Examine the following words and phrases. Choose one of them and write an extended definition of the term in a well-structured paragraph. Be sure your paragraph contains a topic sentence.

1. Natural disaster
2. Soap opera
3. Sorority
4. Hysteria
5. Little League baseball
6. Disgust
7. Health food store
8. Obscenity
9. R-rated movie
10. Workaholic

Paragraph Construction: Orderly Development by Comparison and Contrast

16

IN addition to example and definition, comparison and contrast can also be used to develop a topic sentence into a paragraph. When the writer uses comparison, he concentrates on the similarities between the two persons, places, or things he is writing about. Conversely, when he wants to concentrate on the differences in two persons, places, or things, he uses contrast. If he is concerned with both the similarities and the differences, he uses both comparison and contrast. However, the thrust of a single paragraph is usually in the direction of either the similarities or the differences rather than in the direction of both.

It is important for you to remember that in order to contrast two terms, the two terms must have something in common. For example, it would be difficult, if not impossible, to contrast an elephant and a mousetrap, for these two terms have nothing in common. On the other hand, it would be fairly easy to show the differences between two of your professors, for they do have something in common. Both are people who have chosen teaching as a career. Both are well educated. Both are knowledgeable in their particular fields of study.

By the same token, it would be difficult and quite useless to compare two things that are exactly alike, for a good comparison should be based on some point of difference between the two items.

It is also important to remember that in order to write a good comparison or contrast, you should establish a good basis or several good bases for the discussion of similarities and differences. For example, in writing a paragraph discussing the relative merits of a small car and a large car, you should, at the outset, establish at least two, and preferably three, good bases for the contrast. Three possible bases for such a discussion are expense, comfort, and safety.

After you have established your bases, you must decide on a mode of organization. Two organizational methods are possible. You may choose to discuss the expense, the comfort, and the safety of the small car first and follow this with a discussion of the expense, the comfort, and the safety of the large car. On the other hand, you may choose to discuss first, both cars in terms of expense; second, both cars in terms of comfort; and third, both cars in terms of safety. In a short paragraph either method works well; in an essay the second method is preferable.

Examine the following paragraph:

My Aunt Martha is, to the casual observer, quite different from my Aunt Julie, and yet, except for the differences in physical appearance, ethnic background, and religious affiliation, my two aunts have much in common. The differences between the two are obvious. Aunt Martha is a short, stout, middle-aged, plain-looking brunette, while Aunt Julie is a tall, statuesque, beautiful blonde in her early thirties. Aunt Martha is Italian in origin; Aunt Julie is Norwegian. Aunt Martha is a Roman Catholic; Aunt Julie is a Lutheran. Yet different as they appear to be, my two aunts have much in common. Both are unmarried and fiercely independent. Both are patient and understanding, kind and considerate, so much so that it is frequently difficult to decide which one to go to for comfort, advice, and direction. Both are intelligent and knowledgeable, quick-witted, and clever. But best of all, both Aunt Martha and Aunt Julie love me as a mother loves a daughter.

In this paragraph the similarities between the writer's two aunts are more strikingly significant because of the apparent differences. The casual observer would conclude that the obvious dissimilarities in physical appearance, national origin, and religion would preclude any probability that the two relatives had anything in common. Thus the writer makes the similarities more striking by first showing how different the two aunts are. Notice too that the bases for the contrast are physical appearance, nationality, and religion, whereas the bases for comparison are marital status, personality, mental capacity, and devotion to the writer.

EXERCISE 1
Paragraph Construction: Orderly Development by Comparison and Contrast

Examine the following topics. Choose one of the topics as the subject of a paragraph to be developed by comparison or by contrast. Decide whether you will concentrate on similarities or differences. Then determine what the bases for your comparison or contrast will be. Finally, decide on the method of construction. When you have done all this, write a well-developed comparison or contrast in one well-structured paragraph. Remember that your paragraph must contain a topic sentence. Remember, too, that a comparison will be more effective if based on a difference and that a contrast will be more effective if based on a similarity.

1. Two personal friends
2. Tennis and badminton
3. Handball and racquetball
4. Two high school football (or basketball or track) coaches
5. Contact lenses and eyeglasses
6. Two men (or women) you have dated
7. Water skiing and snow skiing
8. The mountains and the seashore as vacation spots
9. Ice hockey and soccer
10. Two professional football (or basketball, or baseball, or tennis, or ice hockey) players

EXERCISE 2
Paragraph Construction: Orderly Development by Comparison and Contrast

Select one of the following subjects, formulate a topic sentence, establish at least three bases for comparison or contrast, and decide on the mode of construction. Finally develop the topic sentence into a well-structured paragraph concentrating on either similarities or differences.

1. Traditional and contemporary furniture
2. Two popular rock singers
3. Two popular country and western singers
4. Hurricanes and tornadoes
5. Train and air travel
6. Two popular comedians

7. Puppets and marionettes
8. Chess and checkers
9. One-story and two-story homes
10. Water beds and traditional beds

Paragraph Construction: Orderly Development by Cause or Effect

THE fourth method of paragraph development is cause or effect. As a student, you will frequently be called on to discuss the causes or the effects of some event or phenomenon. It is important to remember that causes precede the event and that effects follow the event. If you write a paragraph discussing the reasons something happened, you will be discussing causes. If you write a paragraph discussing the results of some event, you will be discussing effects.

It is sometimes easy to assume that a condition or a circumstance is a cause of a particular event. Therefore, the writer should make certain that he is not confusing causes with conditions and circumstances. For example, in the following paragraph the writer erroneously assumes that certain conditions have caused a particular thing to occur.

> Living in a dormitory causes a student to make poor grades. Because of the noise, he is unable to concentrate. Because of the presence of other students, he finds himself socializing rather than studying. Because of constant interruptions, he finds that he cannot finish an assignment. If a student is to succeed in college, he cannot live in a dormitory.

The writer has confused condition with cause. Certain conditions do, indeed, exist in a dormitory: noise, interruptions, the presence of other students. But these conditions do not necessarily cause a student to make poor grades. Thousands of dormitory students manage to make excellent grades every year in colleges and universities throughout the world.

The writer of the following paragraph is concerned with the same effect as is the writer of the previous paragraph, that is, poor grades. However, instead of confusing conditions with causes, he has analyzed his subject with greater care and has concluded that there are several viable reasons that students make poor grades. He has also concluded that in a single paragraph he cannot discuss all of them; therefore, he chooses the most important. Furthermore, he realizes that he must limit his subject in order to deal with it convincingly in a single paragraph; therefore, he concentrates on failing grades on the part of college freshmen.

Although there are many reasons why college freshmen make failing grades, most failures seem to result from three major causes. The first of these is the student's inability to discipline himself. After considerable dependence on his parents and teachers for making sure that he completes assigned tasks, the freshman suddenly finds himself free of imposed rules and regulations and quite incapable of imposing order on his own life. Another principal cause of freshman failure is poor preparation for advanced-level work. During high school the student may have chosen easy subjects rather than college preparatory courses and consequently is poorly prepared for college-level mathematics, science, and English. Finally, the freshman student may fail because he chooses a major in terms of potential monetary reward rather than in terms of genuine interest and aptitude. Unstimulated and bored by unappealing subject matter, he finds himself unable to succeed. Obviously, then, proper self-discipline, adequate preparation, and sensible career choice would considerably reduce the number of freshman failures in college.

The writer of this paragraph has concentrated on three causes that he considers to be of major importance in determining why college freshmen fail and has presented them with clarity and conviction. These three causes are (1) the student's inability to discipline himself, (2) poor preparation on the part of the student for college-level work, and (3) inappropriate choice of a major on the part of the student.

When you want to write a paragraph developed by effect, you look at the results that come after an event. For example, you may choose to consider the effects of the high price of gasoline and write a paragraph somewhat like the following.

The fact that the price of gasoline has risen dramatically has had three noticeable effects on American drivers. First, most American drivers now look for what is commonly called an economy car when they are in the process of buying a new car. Instead of a large, luxurious car, many buyers prefer a small car that promises good gasoline mileage. Furthermore, many motorists drive their economy cars at a reduced rate of speed in order to get as many miles as possible out of a single gallon of high-priced gasoline. And finally, many Americans restrict their driving to trips that are absolutely necessary in order to reduce their gasoline bills.

In this paragraph the writer has suggested that the three most noticeable effects of the increased cost of gasoline are (1) purchase of economy cars, (2) reduced rate of speed, and (3) elimination of unnecessary motoring.

It is important to remember when using the rhetorical mode called cause or effect that when you are concerned with what comes before and thus produces an event or a phenomenon, you are dealing with causes. When you are concerned with what comes after an event or a phenomenon, you are dealing with results or effects. It is also important to remember not to confuse conditions with causes.

EXERCISE 1
Paragraph Construction: Orderly Development by Cause or Effect

Choose from the topics listed below the one that is of greatest interest to you and decide whether you will use cause or effect to develop the topic into a good paragraph. Then write a topic sentence that clearly states the purpose of your paragraph. Finally, write a paragraph in which you make clear the most important causes or the most important effects of the event or phenomenon you have chosen. Be particularly careful not to confuse conditions or circumstances with causes or effects.

1. Exceeding the speed limit on highways
2. Obesity
3. Social promotion in public schools
4. The generation gap
5. Alcoholism
6. Excessive exposure to the sun
7. Jogging
8. Poor dental hygiene
9. Excessive absence from class
10. Cigarette smoking

Paragraph Construction:
Orderly Development by Cause or Effect

Develop a topic of your own choosing into a paragraph using cause or effect as your rhetorical mode. Be sure to formulate a topic sentence that clearly states the purpose of your paragraph. Choose causes or effects that are important and relevant. Again, do not confuse conditions or circumstances with causes or effects.

Paragraph Construction: Orderly Development by Classification or Division

IN addition to example, definition, comparison and contrast, and cause or effect, a topic sentence can be developed into a paragraph by classification or division. The nature of the topic sentence will determine whether you use classification, which is the process of placing an object or a concept into the general class of which it is a part, or division, which is the process of separating an object or a concept into its basic parts. For example, if we say,

> The foods we eat can be grouped into three large classes: carbohydrates, proteins, and fats.

we are classifying foods; that is, we are placing them into classes. Conversely, if we say,

> Carbohydrates take the form of either starches, sugars, or alcohol.

we are dividing this food group by saying that there are three kinds of carbohydrates; the first is starches, the second, sugars; and the third, alcohol.

In other words, classification involves looking upward to find the larger group to which an object or concept belongs, whereas division involves looking downward to find the parts into which the concept or object can be separated. The direction the writer commits himself to, that is, his decision to use classification or division, is determined by the nature of the topic sentence.

Another important thing to remember when you are developing an idea by classification or division is that there must be clearly defined bases for this mode of development. Examine the following topic sentence.

> According to their training and education, the nurses on the third floor of Santa Rosa Hospital can be grouped into one of two cat-

egories: licensed practical nurses, commonly referred to as LPNs, and registered nurses, known as RNs.

In this topic sentence the nurses are grouped into classes on the basis of their training and education.

The final thing to remember when you are developing an idea by classification or division is that the categories into which you classify a concept, as well as the parts into which you divide a concept, must not overlap; that is, they must be mutually exclusive. For example, there is overlapping in the following classification.

> Many of the immigrants to the United States during the last half of the nineteenth century were from Europe. However, there were some who came from Asia, some from Poland, others from Germany and Iceland, and still others from Japan and China.

The basis for division is, of course, the place the immigrant came from, but the places are not mutually exclusive, for there is overlapping. Poland and Germany are countries in Europe, whereas Japan and China are countries in Asia. The writer should confine himself either to continents of origin or countries of origin, not both. The sentence should read,

> Many of the immigrants to the United States during the last half of the nineteenth century came from either Europe or Asia.

or

> Many of the immigrants to the United States during the last half of the nineteenth century came from Poland and Germany; however, there were others who came from China and Japan.

The following paragraph is developed by classification.

> The three main types of poetry according to content and style are lyric poetry, narrative poetry, and dramatic poetry. Lyric poems express the poet's feelings or emotions, that is, his personal reaction to his subject. Odes, sonnets, elegies, and hymns are considered lyric poems. On the other hand, a narrative poem, which is usually longer than a lyric poem, tells a story. The writer of narrative poetry uses character, setting, and plot to develop his theme. Epics, metrical romances, and ballads are three kinds of narrative poetry. Finally, there is dramatic poetry, in which the author uses dialogue or speech to develop his theme. The dialogue can be actual, as it is in two poetic dramas, T. S. Eliot's *Murder in the Cathedral* and Christopher Marlowe's *The Jew of Malta*, or it can be implied, as it is in Robert Browning's dramatic monologue "My Last Duchess." All poems then can be classified as one of these three types: lyric, narrative, or dramatic.

In this paragraph, the writer classifies poetry into three main categories. He then subdivides each category into its various types.

EXERCISE 1

Paragraph Construction: Orderly Development by Classification or Division

Choose one of the following topics and develop it into a well-structured paragraph by using classification or division. Be sure to determine the basis for your classification or division before you begin to write. Furthermore, be certain that your categories are mutually exclusive; that is, see that they do not overlap. Finally, be sure your paragraph contains a topic sentence.

1. Afternoon television programs
2. The students in your English class
3. Movies
4. Dogs (in terms of their function)
5. Girls to avoid taking out on a date
6. Boys to avoid dating
7. Fraternities
8. Policemen
9. College professors
10. High school principals

EXERCISE 2

Paragraph Construction: Orderly Development by Classification or Division

Using a topic of your own choice, write a well-structured paragraph developed by classification or division. Again, be sure that you determine the basis for your classification or division, that the categories do not overlap, and that your paragraph contains a topic sentence.

Spelling

Diagnostic Spelling Test

Choose the word that is correctly spelled from those that appear in parentheses and write it in the blank at the beginning of each sentence.

1. _____ Ignatius' essay contained four (misspelled, mispelled) words.
2. _____ Dr. Nolander was (dissatisfied, disatisfied) with the plays written by his students.
3. _____ I was (dissappointed, disappointed) when I received a B in the course.
4. _____ The (ceilings, cielings) in the house are ten feet high.
5. _____ If you want to see how many pounds you lose every day, (wiegh, weigh) at the same time every day.
6. _____ Let me give you a (peace, piece) of advice.
7. _____ Grover drove (passed, past) the library three times before he stopped.
8. _____ Hamilton and Burr fought a (duel, dual) to settle their differences.
9. _____ The coal (miners, minors) returned to work today after a prolonged strike.
10. _____ We are required to take four English (coarses, courses).
11. _____ The members of the graduating class will (receive, recieve) their diplomas individually.

12. _____ Do not be (mislead, misled) by his directions.

13. _____ The oasis in the (desert, dessert) was a welcome sight.

14. _____ The (capital, capitol) of New York is Albany.

15. _____ A right (angel, angle) is a 45° (angel, angle).

16. _____ Dr. Dobie, presently a professor of English, was (formerly, formally) a counselor at Lafayette High School.

17. _____ Draw in the (rains, reigns, reins) when you want to stop your horse.

18. _____ (Weather, Whether) conditions are not favorable for fishing.

19. _____ The marriage (rites, rights, writes) were performed in the rose garden.

20. _____ I am (quiet, quite, quit) certain that he is the thief.

21. _____ I keep a daily account of my activities in my (dairy, diary).

22. _____ The sun (shone, shown) brightly after the rain shower.

23. _____ Every one of the professors (except, accept) Mr. Wright will go on vacation this summer.

24. _____ Be sure to get a (receipt, reciept, recipe) when you pay your bill.

25. _____ My friend Donald (dissagreed, disagreed) with everything I said.

26. _____ The (hieght, height, heigth) of the twin towers is over three hundred feet.

27. _____ I would prefer a (stationary, stationery) assignment, for I do not like to move.

28. _____ The children should not be (allowed, aloud) outside after dark.

29. _____ Try not to (lose, loose) your umbrella again today.

30. _____ The burglar will (steel, steal) everything in sight.

31. _____ It is (plain, plane) to see that you are not paying attention.

32. _____ The high school (principle, principal) is a stern disciplinarian.

33. _____ Of the two alternatives you offer, I prefer the (latter, later).

34. _____ (Bare, Bear) in mind that I am opposed to legalized gambling.

35. _____ The architect chose a suitable (sight, site, cite) for the building.

36. _____ Mary, rather (then, than) Martha, would make a good president.
37. _____ (Your, You're) going to be late if you don't hurry.
38. _____ Mr. Baines (proceeded, preceded) his wife as they walked down the aisle.
39. _____ (There, Their, They're) is not much to do on a rainy day.
40. _____ You have to go (through, thorough) two small villages before you get to Crowley.
41. _____ I prefer a (led, lead) pencil to a ballpoint pen.
42. _____ His (birth, berth) is recorded at the Bureau of Vital Statistics.
43. _____ He is (truely, truly) the best friend I have.
44. _____ John Bowles bogied the (nineth, ninth) hole.
45. _____ I must borrow (ninty, ninety) dollars to pay my rent.
46. _____ The two dresses, although not exactly alike, are (similar, similiar) in design.
47. _____ You will need two letters of (recommendation, reccomendation, reccommendation).
48. _____ The car is not (equiped, equipped) with cruise control.
49. _____ The hotel (accommodations, accomodations) were satisfactory.
50. _____ Several (atheletes, athletes) flew to Seattle last week.

Learning to Spell Correctly

The correct spelling of words is not only one of the marks of an educated person; it is also the responsibility of the individual writer. Incorrect spelling often results from the failure of the individual to pronounce words correctly. Therefore, it is important for the writer to pronounce clearly and accurately all the words that he uses. Another cause of misspelling is the writer's failure to see the difference between words that are similar in sound and spelling but that have different meanings. Consequently, it is important for the writer to distinguish between such words and to spell these words according to their meanings. Furthermore, misspelling can result from the writer's inability to recognize prefixes, roots, and suffixes. Once this recognition takes place and a few simple rules governing the addition of prefixes and suffixes to the root are mastered, you will eliminate many incorrectly spelled words from your writing. Finally, misspelling is often the result of the writer's failure to learn a few basic rules that will help him to spell correctly. Therefore, it is important to learn and apply these rules in order to become a good speller.

While you as a student are mastering these techniques for improving your spelling, you should keep a list of all the words that are marked misspelled on your papers. By learning to spell these words correctly, you will take a giant step in the direction of correct spelling. Four other steps in this direction—(1) correct pronunciation as a means of correct spelling, (2) distinguishing between words with similar sounds and spellings but with different meanings, (3) adding prefixes and suffixes to the root form of the word, and (4) forming plurals—will lead you closer and closer to your goal of acquiring one of the marks of an educated person.

CORRECT PRONUNCIATION AS A MEANS OF CORRECT SPELLING

The following words are frequently misspelled because the writer omits a sound when pronouncing the words. You should practice saying these words aloud, being careful to enunciate the sounds represented by the italicized letters. Repeated practice in sounding out these letters should result in increased awareness of the correct spelling of many problem words.

accident*a*lly (al)
ane*c*dote (c)
apost*ro*phe (ro)
ar*c*tic (c)
auxil*i*ary (i)
bach*e*lor (e)
bat*te*ry (te)
clima*c*tic (c)
deteri*or*ate (or)
di*ph*theria (ph = f)
do*r*mitory (r)
enviro*n*ment (n)
incident*a*lly (al)
lab*o*ratory (o)
len*g*th (g)
lib*r*ary (r)
lit*e*rature (e)
mathe*m*atics (e)
med*i*eval (i)
occasion*a*lly (al)

proba*b*ly (b)
quan*ti*ty (t)
reco*g*nition (g)
reco*g*nize (g)
sal*a*ry (a)
san*d*wich (d)
sec*r*etary (r)
sev*e*ral (e)
soph*o*more (o)
super*in*tendent (in)
suppose*d* to (d)
su*r*prise (r)
tempe*r*ature (e)
tempe*r*ence (e)
use*d* to (d)
valu*a*ble (a)
vege*t*ables (e)
vet*e*ran (e)
veter*i*narian (i)

Sometimes the addition rather than the omission of a sound in pronouncing a word results in the misspelling of a word. Again, repeated practice in saying these words aloud and omitting the extra sounds should result in an increased awareness of the correct spelling of many problem words. Such words include

athlete *not* ath*e*lete
athletics *not* ath*e*letics
exercise *not* ex*c*ercise
grievous *not* griev*i*ous
height *not* height*h*
mischievous *not* mischiev*i*ous
suffrage *not* suff*e*rage

Finally, some words are simply mispronounced and are, therefore, spelled incorrectly. Practice the correct pronunciation of the following words, paying attention to the italicized letters. Such practice will result in the correct spelling of these problem words.

apost*ro*phe	pe*r*haps
*cal*vary	pe*r*spiration
cav*al*ry	p*re*fer
int*ro*duce	p*re*serve
irrel*ev*ant	p*ro*fessor
kinderga*r*ten	pro*nun*ciation
mainte*n*ance	sim*i*lar
opp*or*tunity	undoub*ted*ly

DISTINGUISHING BETWEEN WORDS WITH SIMILAR SOUNDS AND SPELLINGS BUT WITH DIFFERENT MEANINGS

The following words are often misspelled because the writer fails to choose the word that correctly conveys his meaning. Study the words in each group, being careful to learn the distinctions between the words in terms of meaning. (This list does not exhaust all possibilities; it merely includes the most common misspellings resulting from confusion of meaning. Furthermore, the definitions do not exhaust all nuances of meaning; rather, they include meanings most often used and confused.)

1. *Accept, except. Accept* is a verb meaning *to take or to endure willingly.*

Ex.: John *accepted* the honor with obvious pleasure.
The criminal *accepted* his punishment stoically.

Except is a verb or preposition having to do with *exclusion*.

Ex.: Because his grade-point average was low, the honor society *excepted* his name from the list of potential members.
Everyone in our class *except* John was invited to the dance.

2. *Affect, effect. Affect* is a verb meaning *to exert influence*.

Ex.: His bad health *affected* his work.

Effect can be used as a verb, meaning *to cause to happen*, or as a noun, meaning *result*.

Ex.: The new speed limit has *effected* a reduction in car accidents.
Air pollution has had many undesirable *effects* on the health of the citizens of this community.

3. *All ready, already. All ready* means *completely prepared* or *finished*.

Ex.: He had his term paper *all ready* a week before it was due.

Already means *before some past, present, or future time*.

Ex.: It is *already* time for final exams.

4. *All together, altogether. All together* means the *involvement of a group acting together*.

Ex.: The crew rowed the boat *all together*.

Altogether means *completely* or *entirely*.

Ex.: Your answer is *altogether* incorrect.

5. *Altar, alter. Altar* is a noun meaning *a place of sacrifice or worship*.

Ex.: The *altar* of the church was inlaid with ivory and gold.

Alter is a verb meaning *to change*.

Ex.: Your behavior will not *alter* my decision.

6. *Aloud, allowed. Aloud* is an adverb meaning *the opposite of silently*.

Ex.: Professor Baines read the passage *aloud*.

Allowed is the past tense of the verb *to allow*, meaning *to permit*.

Ex.: Dr. Jones *allowed* me to take a make-up test.

7. *Allusion, illusion. Allusion* is a noun meaning *an indirect reference to literature, history, and the like*.

Ex.: Hemingway's title *For Whom the Bell Tolls* is an *allusion* to a passage in John Donne's "No Man Is an Island."

Illusion is a noun meaning *an appearance that is distorted or false.*

Ex.: A mirage is an *illusion.*

8. *Angel, angle. Angel* is a noun referring to *a spirit, a heavenly being, or one resembling such a spirit or being.*

Ex.: *Angels* in heaven are sometimes pictured as spirits in white robes playing golden harps.

Angle is a noun referring to the *point of convergence of two straight lines,* as well as a noun meaning *point of view.*

Ex.: An *angle* can be an obtuse *angle,* an acute *angle,* or a right *angle.*
We must look at the problem from all *angles.*

9. *Berth, birth. Berth* is a noun meaning *a place to rest or sleep.*

Ex.: I prefer the upper *berth* in a sleeper on a train.

Birth is a noun meaning *the act of bringing forth, especially of bringing into life.*

Ex.: My *birth* is recorded in the Bureau of Vital Statistics.

10. *Brake, break. Brake* is a noun or a verb that has to do with *stopping or halting.*

Ex.: Faulty *brakes* caused the driver to run the stop sign.
His failure to *brake* the car rapidly caused the accident.

Break is a verb or a noun having to do with *separating into smaller pieces* or *interrupting.*

Ex.: I did not intend to *break* the vase.
Diplomatic arrogance caused the *break* in friendly relations between the two countries.

11. *Capital, capitol. Capital* is a noun meaning *the city where the seat of government is located* or the *net worth of an individual or company. Capital* can also be used as an adjective meaning *very serious* or *involving execution.*

Ex.: Baton Rouge is the *capital* of Louisiana.
He invested all his *capital* in stocks and bonds.
Capital punishment has not been outlawed in the United States.

Capitol is a noun meaning the *building in which a state or national legislative body holds its meetings.*

Ex.: The architect who designed the *capitol* in Austin, Texas, modeled it after the United States *Capitol* in Washington, D.C.

12. *Censor, censure. Censor* is a verb meaning *to examine closely in order to eliminate if objectionable.*

    Ex.: During World War II, authorities were careful to *censor* all letters sent to or from overseas addresses.

    Censure is a verb meaning *to chastise or condemn.*

    Ex.: Divorce is *censured* by many religions.

13. *Cite, sight, site. Cite* is a verb meaning *to quote, to summon for a court appearance,* or *to speak of in formal praise.*

    Ex.: Passages from Shakespeare's sonnets are frequently *cited* by my English teacher.
    My father has never been *cited* for a traffic violation.
    His many services to his community were *cited* as evidence of his good citizenship.

    Sight is a noun or verb having to do with *visual perception.*

    Ex.: The *sight* of the effects of the tornado appalled me.
    The captain of the shipwrecked vessel finally *sighted* land.

    Site is a noun meaning *location.*

    Ex.: The town council cannot decide on a *site* for the new court-house.

14. *Close, clothes, cloths. Close* is a verb meaning *to shut, to end or finish;* a noun meaning *the end;* and an adjective meaning *intimate.*

    Ex.: *Close* the door.
    Will you please *close* the discussion?
    The passage that brought the play to a *close* was unduly sentimental.
    My sister and I have a *close* relationship.

    Clothes is a noun meaning *wearing apparel or garments.*

    Ex.: Her *clothes* are always representative of the latest fashions.

    Cloths is the plural of *cloth,* which means *fabric or a fabric used for a specific purpose.*

    Ex.: Separate the towels from the wash *cloths* before you wash them.

15. *Coarse, course. Coarse* is an adjective having to do with *inferior quality, rough surface,* or *crude language and manners.*

Ex.: Tin is considered a *coarse* metal.
　　Linen is *coarser* than silk.
　　My parents objected to his *coarse* language.

Course is a noun meaning *path, direction of flight, or an academic or vocational subject.*

Ex.: The hunter followed a direct *course* through the swamp.
　　Several math *courses* are required in my curriculum.

16. *Complement, compliment. Complement* is a verb or a noun having to do with *completing.*

Ex.: The twins *complement* each other; what one lacks, the other has.
　　Angle ACD is a *complement* to angle DCB; together they form a right angle.

Compliment is a noun or a verb having to do with *admiring or praising.*

Ex.: The current Miss America has received many *compliments* on her beauty.
　　The judges *complimented* Miss America on her unusual and varied talents.

17. *Conscience, conscious. Conscience* is a noun that means *the sense of virtue together with the felt need to be or do good.*

Ex.: My *conscience* told me to return the money.

Conscious is an adjective having to do with *awareness.*

Ex.: I was *conscious* of the fact that I was about to fail the course.

18. *Dairy, diary. Dairy* is a noun referring to *a place where milk and milk products are produced.*

Ex.: Call the *dairy* and ask them to stop our milk delivery.

Diary is a noun referring to *a day-by-day account of events or feelings.*

Ex.: Samuel Pepys' *diary* has been an invaluable source of information about seventeenth-century England.

19. *Desert, dessert. Desert* is a noun meaning *a dry or arid region.* It is also a verb meaning *to abandon.*

Ex.: *Deserts* can become productive through irrigation.
　　His mother *deserted* him when he was a child.

Dessert is a noun meaning *the last course of a meal.*

Ex.: The *desserts* I like are chocolate pudding, pecan pie, and strawberry ice cream.

20. *Device, devise. Device* is a noun meaning *something that is contrived* or *something that is made for a particular purpose.*

   Ex.: He invented several *devices* for easing the discomfort of broken bones.

   Devise is a verb meaning *to formulate in the mind* or *to invent.*

   Ex.: The exterminator *devised* a new way of getting rid of termites.

21. *Dual, duel. Dual* is an adjective implying *two.*

   Ex.: Her son's *dual* personality often confuses Mrs. Dobie.

   Duel is a noun implying *the confrontation between two people who carry weapons.*

   Ex.: Settling differences by fighting a *duel* is no longer a common practice.

22. *Dying, dyeing. Dying* is *the act of ceasing to live.*

   Ex.: As a result of the accident, my uncle is slowly *dying.*

   Dyeing is *the act of changing the color of an object.*

   Ex.: This tailor shop specializes in cleaning and *dyeing* clothing.

23. *Emigrate, immigrate. Emigrate* is a verb meaning *to leave a country permanently.*

   Ex.: Many families *emigrated* from Ireland during the nineteenth century.

   Immigrate is a verb meaning *to enter a country for the purpose of settling.*

   Ex.: My forefathers *immigrated* to this country from Europe.

24. *Eminent, imminent. Eminent* is an adjective implying *importance or renown.*

   Ex.: Louis Pasteur was an *eminent* scientist.

   Imminent is an adjective meaning *about to take place.*

   Ex.: The threatening clouds indicated that a tornado was *imminent.*

25. *Fair, fare. Fair* is a noun meaning *festival* and an adjective meaning *without prejudice.*

   Ex.: We attended the state *fair* in Baton Rouge.
   My professor is always *fair* in his evaluation of students.

Fare is a noun meaning *the amount charged for transportation.*

Ex.: The air *fare* from Houston to San Francisco is over three hundred dollars.

26. *Formally, formerly. Formally* is an adverb meaning *with great dignity or ceremony* or *according to the proper rules and customs.*

Ex.: The mayor *formally* announced his candidacy for governor at the Chamber of Commerce banquet.

Formerly is an adverb meaning *previously or before a certain time.*

Ex.: The governor was *formerly* the mayor of our town.

27. *Forth, fourth. Forth* is an adverb meaning *onward, forward,* or *outward.*

Ex.: Going *forth* into the world to make one's own living can be a satisfying experience.

Fourth is the noun *deriving from the numeral four, indicating position or portion.*

Ex.: My sister won *fourth* place in the state spelling competition.
May I buy a *fourth* of a pound of butter?

28. *Hear, here. Hear* is a verb meaning *to be aware of something through the ears.*

Ex.: After the operation on his eardrums, the child was able to *hear.*

Here is an adverb meaning *at this place.*

Ex.: The chair belongs *here* by the window.

29. *Hole, whole. Hole* is a noun meaning *a cavity or opening.*

Ex.: The explosion left a huge *hole* in the street.

Whole is an adjective meaning entire and a noun meaning *the entire thing.*

Ex.: The dog ate the *whole* roast.
The *whole* is the sum of all its parts.

30. *Its, it's. Its* is *the third-person singular neuter possessive pronoun.*

Ex.: After five hours, the hurricane lost *its* force.

It's is *the contraction for it is.*

Ex.: *It's* too early to determine the results of the experiment.

31. *Know, no. Know* is the verb meaning *to be aware of, to understand, to discern, to be acquainted with.*

Ex.: I *know* that it will be difficult to pass the course.

No is a word that expresses *negation.*

Ex.: I have *no* idea where I put my books.

32. *Later, latter. Later* is an adverb meaning *at some future time.*

Ex.: Because Mr. Gray is ill today, he will see you *later* in the week.

Latter is a noun or an adjective meaning *the second in a series of two.*

Ex.: I think the *latter* can be more easily effected.

33. *Lead, led. Lead* is a noun referring to *a metallic element. Lead* is also the present tense of the verb meaning *to give direction by going first.*

Ex.: *Lead* is used in pencils.

Led is the past tense of the verb *to lead,* meaning *to give direction by going first.*

Ex.: During the final campaign of the war, Sergeant Max *led* his troops into action.

34. *Lightening, lightning. Lightening* means *making less heavy.*

Ex.: *Lightening* the load in your knapsack will enable you to move faster.

Lightning means a flash of light during an electrical storm.

Ex.: *Lightning* and thunder terrified the little girls.

35. *Loose, lose. Loose* means *not tight.*

Ex.: The Roman toga was a *loose* garment.

Lose is a verb meaning *to fail to keep, to fail to win, to fail to keep track of.*

Ex.: A person can *lose* a great amount of money as a result of a bad investment.
Athletes should learn to *lose* gracefully.
My father *loses* one or two balls every time he plays golf.

36. *Passed, past. Passed* is the past tense of the verb *to pass,* which means *to issue a judgment in a court of law, to successfully complete a course, to overtake another person,* and *to transfer.*

Ex.: Judge Everett *passed* sentence on the convicted murderer.
My brother *passed* geometry with an A but failed algebra.
The Jaguar *passed* the Mercedes with no trouble.
At his father's death, the property *passed* to John.

Past can be used as an adjective denoting *something that has occurred before the present* and as a noun indicating *time gone by*.

Ex.: For the *past* three years, I have been attempting to succeed as a student.
The policeman drove *past* me and waved.
I do not concern myself with the *past,* only with the present and the future.

37. *Precede, proceed. Precede* is a verb meaning *to go before*.

Ex.: Husbands usually *precede* their wives in death.

Proceed is a verb meaning *to go forward*.

Ex.: The hikers will *proceed* no farther until the storm ends.

38. *Principal, principle. Principal,* when used as an adjective, means *most important;* when used as a noun, it means *headmaster* or *administrator of a school*.

Ex.: The *principal* reason for my failure in school was bad study habits.
The *principal* of the high school in our town has good rapport with both his faculty and his students.

Principle is a noun meaning *a basic law or tenet* or *a code of conduct*.

Ex.: Newton discovered the *principle* of gravity.
Do not expect me to adopt your *principles* of behavior.

39. *Prophecy, prophesy. Prophecy* is a noun meaning *an announcement concerning the future*.

Ex.: The clairvoyant's *prophecy* concerning the attempted assassination of the president turned out to be a hoax.

Prophesy is a verb meaning *to predict the future*.

Ex.: Attempts to *prophesy* the future are usually dismal failures.

40. *Quiet, quite. Quiet* is an adjective implying *the absence of noise, commotion, confusion, and so on*.

Ex.: Early morning is a *quiet* time of the day.

Quite is an adjective meaning *completely* or *without doubt*.

Ex.: I am *quite* certain that I will be unable to attend the banquet.

41. *Right, rite, wright, write. Right* is an adjective meaning *correct*, an adjective meaning *not left*, a noun meaning *a just claim*, and a verb meaning *to correct a wrong.*

> Ex.: Your answer is *right*.
> Raise your *right* hand.
> You have no *right* to question his motives.
> The knights of yore attempted to *right* wrongs.

Rite is a noun meaning *ceremony.*

> Ex.: The wedding *rite* will be performed in the spacious garden.

Wright is a noun meaning *a skilled worker.* The word is usually used in combination with the name of the craft.

> Ex.: In times of war many *shipwrights* are employed in naval yards.

Note: A writer of a drama is a playwright, not a *playwrite.*
Write is a verb meaning *to place words upon paper.*

> Ex.: I usually do not *write* letters to my parents; rather, I talk to them by phone.

42. *Shone, shown. Shone* is the past tense of the verb to shine, meaning *to sparkle or glitter.*

> Ex.: The beam of the flashlight *shone* through the murky darkness.

Shown is the past participle of the verb *to show*, meaning *to exhibit or demonstrate.*

> Ex.: The paintings *shown* at the art museum last week were purchased by Stanley McFadden.

43. *Soar, sore. Soar* is a verb meaning *to go aloft* or *to go high into the air.*

> Ex.: Hang gliders, as they *soar* through the air, are beautiful to see.

Sore is an adjective meaning *painful* and a noun meaning *an infected opening in the skin.*

> Ex.: My right knee has been *sore* ever since the accident.
> Open *sores* appeared on my hands as a result of the infection.

44. *Stationary, stationery. Stationary* is an adjective meaning *fixed, incapable of being moved.*

> Ex.: The chairs are *stationary* because they are bolted to the floor.

Stationery is a noun meaning *paper on which letters are written.*

Ex.: The letterhead on his *stationery* was designed by Cartier.

45. *Steal, steel. Steal* is a verb meaning *to take something illegally* or *to move secretly or without being noticed.*

Ex.: His intense hunger made him *steal* the food.
This player can often *steal* a base.

Steel is a noun referring to *something hard or strong* or a noun meaning *an alloy of iron and carbon. Steel* can also be used as an adjective referring to *something hard or strong.*

Ex.: He has nerves of *steel.*
His anchor is made of *steel.*
Steel instruments are long-lasting.

46. *Than, then. Than* is the word used in a *comparison.*

Ex.: I am older *than* you are.

Then is an adverb indicating *time.*

Ex.: Go to the corner, *then* turn right and go two blocks.

47. *There, their, they're. There* is an adverb meaning *in that position* or *not here.*

Ex.: I'm not sure it's safe to go *there* at this time of night.

Their is the *third-person plural possessive pronoun.*

Ex.: Most of *their* time was taken in peeling rather than in eating the shrimp.

They're is the contraction of *they are.*

Ex.: The Joneses called to say *they're* coming immediately.

48. *Threw, through. Threw* is the past tense of the verb *to throw,* meaning *to toss.*

Ex.: The pitcher *threw* a wild ball and lost the ball game.

Through is a preposition meaning *by way of or because of.*

Ex.: The sailors steered the ship *through* the dangerous channel.
He lost his business *through* negligence.

49. *To, two, too. To* is a preposition meaning *toward or in the direction of.*

Ex.: He will go *to* the convention in Dallas.

Two is a number.

Ex.: A *two*-dollar bill is a rarity.

Too means *also*.

Ex.: I, *too*, will get my degree in June.

50. *Weak, week. Weak* is an adjective meaning *not strong.*

Ex.: As a result of his illness, my father was *weak* for a month.

Week is a noun indicating *a period of seven days.*

Ex.: Easter holidays will last for a *week*.

51. *Weather, whether. Weather* can be used as a noun meaning *climatic conditions,* or as a verb meaning *to endure,* or as an adjective referring to *climatic conditions.*

Ex.: The *weather* was ideal for the fishing trip.
    The house is built to *weather* almost any kind of storm.
    Weather conditions can be unstable at this time of year.

Whether is a word *usually followed by or indicating an alternative.*

Ex.: I do not know *whether* or not the major candidate will appear at the convention.

52. *Whose, who's. Whose* is a relative pronoun denoting *possession.*

Ex.: This is the man *whose* watch was stolen.

Who's is the contraction for *who is.*

Ex.: This is the athlete *who's* most likely to win the gold medal.

53. *Your, you're. Your* is the *second-person possessive pronoun.*

Ex.: *Your* new dress is very becoming.

You're is the contraction for *you are.*

Ex.: *You're* going to be late if you don't hurry.

ADDING PREFIXES AND SUFFIXES TO THE ROOT FORM OF THE WORD

The Addition of Prefixes

The addition of such prefixes as *mis, dis, im, in,* and *un* does not change the spelling of the root word.

mis + spell = misspell
mis + adventure = misadventure

```
mis + lay = mislay
mis + treat = mistreat
dis + appoint = disappoint
dis + advantage = disadvantage
dis + approve = disapprove
im + mortal = immortal
im + material = immaterial
im + mature = immature
im + mobile = immobile
in + numerable = innumerable
in + most = inmost
un + necessary = unnecessary
un + natural = unnatural
un + numbered = unnumbered
un + official = unofficial
```

The Addition of Suffixes

A few rules, when learned and applied, will help you spell correctly words that are formed by adding a suffix to the root form of the word. This series of rules does not by any means exhaust the entire list of rules applicable to the addition of suffixes. You can consult your dictionary for additional rules.

Words Ending in Silent *e*

The final *e* is dropped before suffixes beginning with a vowel and retained before suffixes beginning with a consonant.

come + ing = coming	come + ly = comely
care + ing = caring	care + less = careless
	care + ful = careful
curve + ing = curving	curve + some = curvesome
state + ing = stating	state + ment = statement
imagine + ing = imagining	imagine + less = imagineless
place + ed = placed	place + ment = placement
name + ing = naming	name + less = nameless

Exceptions:

```
true + ly = truly
awe + ful = awful
dye + ing = dyeing
nine + th = ninth
courage + ous = courageous
notice + able = noticeable
```

Words Ending in a Final Single Consonant Preceded by a Single Vowel

If the word has only one syllable or if the word ends in a stressed syllable, double the final consonant before a suffix beginning with a vowel; but do not double the final consonant before a suffix beginning with a consonant.

```
stop + ing = stopping
sit + ing = sitting
get + ing = getting
let + ing = letting
confer + ing = conferring
regret + ing = regretting
equip + ed = equipped
equip + ment = equipment
bad + ly = badly
confer + ment = conferment
```

Words Ending in a Final Single Consonant Preceded by a Double Vowel

If the word has only one syllable or if the word ends in a stressed syllable, do not double the final consonant before a suffix beginning with a vowel.

```
stoop + ing = stooping
scoop + ing = scooping
tool + ing = tooling
drool + ing = drooling
```

Words Ending in a Double Consonant

If the word ends in two consonants, the final consonant is not doubled before adding a suffix.

```
part + ing = parting
resign + ing = resigning
assist + ed = assisted
perform + ing = performing
govern + ed = governed
```

Words Ending in Final *y* Preceded by a Consonant

The final *y* is usually changed to *i* before suffixes, except those beginning with an *i*.

```
beauty + ful = beautiful
ready + ness = readiness
defy + ance = defiance
defy + ing = defying
mercy + less = merciless
happy + ly = happily
modify + er = modifier
modify + ing = modifying
```

FORMING PLURALS

Most nouns are pluralized by adding *s* to the singular.

> hat—hats
> boy—boys
> picture—pictures
> girl—girls
> lesson—lessons

Nouns ending in *s, sh, ch, x,* or *z* form their plurals by adding *es* to the singular. Exception: Nouns ending in *ch* that has the *k* sound are pluralized by adding *s*.

> box—boxes
> grass—grasses
> latch—latches
> kiss—kisses

Nouns ending in *o* preceded by a consonant add *es* to form the plural; if the *o* is preceded by a vowel, add *s*.

> ratio—ratios
> radio—radios
> hero—heroes

Exceptions:

> piano—pianos
> banjo—banjos
> photo—photos
> auto—autos

Most nouns ending in *f* or *fe* add an *s* to form the plural.

> proof—proofs
> safe—safes

Some nouns ending in *f* or *fe* change the *f* or *fe* to *v* before adding *es*.

> knife—knives
> wolf—wolves
> thief—thieves

DISTINGUISHING BETWEEN *IE* AND *EI*

A good rule to remember in distinguishing between *ie* and *ei* is

> *i* before *e*
> except after *c*
> or when sounded like *a*
> as in *neighbor* and *weigh*

believe
piece
relieve
conceive
deceive
sleigh

Exceptions:

their
either
leisure
seize
weird

The rules and suggestions in this chapter, when mastered and applied, will help you to eliminate many errors in your spelling. These suggestions and rules, however, are by no means comprehensive; therefore, you should make a habit of consulting your dictionary if you have any doubt about the correct spelling of a word. Furthermore, if you are interested in learning additional rules about correct spelling, you should look in your dictionary for the section entitled "Spelling" and study the rules outlined in this section.

EXERCISE 2
Mastery Test on Spelling

Select the correctly spelled word from those that appear in parentheses and write it in the blank preceding each sentence.

1. _____ I prefer the lower (birth, berth) when sleeping on a train.

2. _____ The total (affects, effects) of nuclear radiation have not as yet been determined.

3. _____ Our botany class went on a (feild, field) trip last Friday.

4. _____ I was (embarassed, embarrassed) by his constant attention.

5. _____ I will apply for a (goverment, government) job after I graduate.

6. _____ Try to learn the correct (pronounciation, pronunciation) of the words so that you will spell them correctly.

7. _____ The Indian (cheif, chief) was unwilling to sign the treaty.

8. _____ In the movie the hero finally conquered the (villain, villian).

9. _____ You are altogether (to, too, two) lenient.

10. _____ The carpenter held the piece of lumber in the (vice, vise).

11. _____ My mother gave me a (suprise, surprise) birthday party.

12. _____ You will (undoubtedly, undoubtably) want the weekend free.

13. _____ Do not leave (until, untill) I return.

14. _____ My brother Steve recently became a (veterinarian, veternarian).

15. _____ Be sure to (separate, seperate) the oranges from the lemons.

16. _____ James found it (unecessary, unnecessary) to hire a helper.

17. _____ When I become a (sophmore, sophomore), I will select a major.

18. _____ Poetry has regular (rhythm, rythm, rhithm); prose does not.

19. _____ I am required to take two courses in (mathmatics, mathematics).

20. _____ You may be denied the (priviledge, privilege) of attending the concert.

21. _____ We have two (playwrites, playwrights) on our faculty.

22. _____ Babies should be innoculated against (diphtheria, diphtheria).

23. _____ The (enviromental, environmental) agency did not enforce the laws.

24. _____ My fishing boat has (duel, dual) motors.

25. _____ The United States relies heavily on (foriegn, foreign) oil.

26. _____ My friend was (dissappointed, disappointed) when you failed to arrive.

27. _____ The (govenor, governor) of our state is a Republican.

28. _____ It is against the law to sell beer to (minors, miners).

29. _____ The (stationery, stationary) you used to write your letters was soiled.

30. _____ Several (mathmatics, mathematics) professors resigned last spring.

31. _____ (Losing, loosing) one's textbooks can be expensive.

32. _____ The bull lost (its, it's) head and dashed madly around the arena.
33. _____ The regiment went (forth, fourth) into battle.
34. _____ (Breath, Breathe) deeply while I listen to your heartbeat.
35. _____ Put the (bridal, bridle) on the horse before you mount him.
36. _____ The (capitol, capital) of the United States houses the Senate and the House of Representatives.
37. _____ Put your contribution on the church (alter, altar).
38. _____ The judge (complimented, complemented) Miss America's unusual talent.
39. _____ (Climatic, Climactic) conditions caused the explorers to return to camp.
40. _____ He is uncertain about (weather, whether) to go or not.
41. _____ The sheep will be (sheared, sheered) in the spring.
42. _____ The (Statue, Stature) of Liberty was given to the United States by France.
43. _____ Your (strenth, strength) is quite unusual for a man of your size.
44. _____ The student (whose, who's) book you found lives in Brown Dormitory.
45. _____ During the storm his clothes were torn to (peaces, pieces).
46. _____ The (atheletic, athletic) department will sponsor the tournament.
47. _____ Several words were (mispelled, misspelled) in your essay.
48. _____ A flash of (lightening, lightning) is usually followed by thunder.
49. _____ The lieutenant (led, lead) his men into combat.
50. _____ (Medieval, medival) history and literature have much in common.

Punctuation

Diagnostic Test

Punctuate the following sentences correctly.

1. If you listen you will learn.
2. He came he saw he conquered.
3. The dog cold and hungry appeared at my back door.
4. My brother prefers hamburgers my sister hot dogs.
5. The teacher asked whether or not we wanted to go on a field trip.
6. When you have answered all the questions you may leave.
7. Dr. Fields walked to the podium looked at his audience and began his address.
8. I will leave whenever you are ready.
9. Ronald Reagan president of the United States is a Republican.
10. James Nixon Jr M D is my only brothers doctor.
11. Although Horace does not take copious notes he does well on his tests.
12. I will not vote for the bill nor will I agree to a compromise.
13. You must take the medicine or you will suffer the consequences.
14. The band concert was canceled when the tornado warning was issued.
15. I will visit Miami when I go to Florida.
16. The coach announced that Bill won the gold medal that George won the silver medal and that Tom won the bronze medal.

17. I am catching a cold therefore I will be unable to attend the football game.
18. This salad contains lettuce tomatoes green peppers and celery.
19. John Mary James and Jane left yesterday for Europe.
20. My granddaughter is a quiet sensitive individual.
21. Few short men become good basketball players.
22. Mary I want to recommend you for the honors program.
23. While looking for a westward route to India Columbus discovered America.
24. On July 4 1776 the American colonies declared their independence from England.
25. Nancy Reagan wearing a formal evening gown designed by Georgia Yves walked regally into the ballroom.
26. Abraham Lincoln who was born in a log cabin eventually occupied the White House.
27. My new address is 204 Summit Lane Los Angeles California.
28. By the way where are you going on your vacation?
29. Dr. Hirt unlike Dr. Pauley is a right-wing conservative.
30. The bananas not the peaches are spoiled and need to be thrown away.
31. The soldiers were poorly trained consequently they lost the battle.
32. My grandmother taught me to knit to crochet and to embroider.
33. I wonder however if he is as intelligent as he claims to be.
34. On Saturday my fathers chores include mowing the grass clipping the hedge and pulling the weeds from the garden.
35. Dr. Fontenot has won prizes for his poetry his short stories and his essays.
36. I will celebrate my next birthday on August 13 1983.
37. Pleased to be chosen chairman Mrs White thanked the members of the nominating committee.
38. Out-of-state students not Texas residents are required to take entrance examinations at Austin State College.
39. You must have a parking permit or you will not be allowed to park your car on campus.
40. Generally speaking students at this university are friendly and courteous.
41. The Spaniards came to America in search of gold the English came in search of religious freedom.
42. Although his father is a United States senator Gerald has no interest in politics.
43. Tulips roses azaleas and camellias grow in my mothers garden.

44. English literature not English grammar is my favorite subject.
45. Columbus ships were called the Niña the Pinta and the Santa Maria.
46. My only brothers favorite spectator sport is football.
47. The childrens playground was under water after the rain.
48. Harrys and Cliffs cars were destroyed during the tornado.
49. The insurance company was responsible for the damages however it was reluctant to pay the full amount charged for repairs.
50. Neither rain sleet nor snow shall delay my trip to Chicago.

Learning to Punctuate

In order to be a good writer, a person must learn to punctuate his sentences correctly. That is, he must learn how to use periods, question marks, exclamation marks, commas, colons, semicolons, hyphens, dashes, parentheses, brackets, apostrophes, and quotation marks. This lesson will not deal with all these marks of punctuation but rather with the most frequently used; namely, the comma, the semicolon, the apostrophe, and the period.

THE COMMA

The most frequent punctuation error is, in all probability, in the use of the comma. This is true mainly because the comma is used more frequently than any other single mark of punctuation. Errors occur not only in the omission of commas but also in the unnecessary use of commas. First, then, the student should learn a few basic rules governing the occasions when a comma is necessary. A general rule to remember is that commas are used to set off or separate certain words, phrases, and clauses in a sentence.

1. When two independent clauses are joined by short conjunctions such as *and, but, or, nor, for,* and *yet,* a comma is placed after the first independent clause.

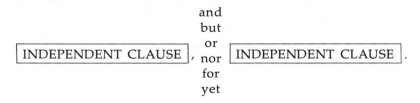

(1) The wind stopped blowing , and the snow started falling .

(2) Mrs. Byrne wanted to vacation in Canada , but her husband preferred Mexico .

(3) You must take the medicine , or you will suffer severe pain .

(4) I will not agree to John's plan , nor will I support your alternative .

(5) Jane could not ski , for she had broken her ankle .

(6) Dr. Fields made no comment , yet it was obvious he disagreed .

In the preceding sentences the group of words before as well as the group of words following the short conjunctions *and, but, or, nor, for,* and *yet* are independent clauses; that is, they make complete sense when standing alone. When such complete statements are joined by short conjunctions, a comma is placed after the first statement.

2a. When a dependent adverbial clause precedes the independent clause in a sentence, a comma is placed after the dependent clause. A dependent adverbial clause is a group of words containing a subject and a predicate verb that answers the questions "How?" "When?" "Where?" and "For what reason?" These dependent adverbial clauses cannot stand alone; that is, they depend on the independent clause for complete meaning. Such dependent adverbial clauses are introduced by words like *before, after, because, since, when, whenever, while, if, as, although,* and *wherever.*

DEPENDENT ADVERBIAL CLAUSE , INDEPENDENT CLAUSE .

(1) Before Mr. Edwards was governor , he was mayor of our town .

(2) After you finish the examination , you may leave .

(3) Because I could not solve the problem , I failed the test .

(4) Since Dr. Cain has been head of the department , she has not had a vacation .

(5) When the storm clouds appeared , the picnic was canceled .

(6) [Whenever I feel depressed] , [I buy a new dress] .

(7) [While I am in California] , [I will visit San Francisco] .

(8) [If I pass logic] , [I will graduate in June] .

(9) [As the band marched by] , [the crowd cheered] .

(10) [Although I failed the final] , [I passed the course] .

(11) [Wherever I went] , [my dog followed me] .

2b. If a dependent adverbial clause follows the main clause, a comma is not used to separate the two clauses.

    (1) Mr. Edwards was the mayor of our town before he became governor.

    (2) You may leave after you finish the examination.

    (3) I failed the test because I could not solve the problem.

    (4) Dr. Cain has not had a vacation since she became head of the department.

    (5) The picnic was canceled when the storm clouds appeared.

    (6) I buy a new dress whenever I feel depressed.

    (7) I will visit San Francisco while I am in California.

    (8) I will graduate in June if I pass logic.

    (9) The crowd cheered as the band marched by.

    (10) I passed the course although I failed the final examination.

    (11) My dog followed me wherever I went.

3. Words, phrases, and clauses in a series of three or more are separated by commas.

    (1) [John] , [Jane] , [Ruth] , and [Bert] are vacationing in Florida.

    (2) The fans [laughed] , [danced] , [yelled] , and [sang] at the concert.

    (3) Waldorf salad is made of [apples] , [celery] , and [walnuts] .

    (4) Mr. Byrne walked [up the stairs] , [down the hall] , and [into his office] .

    (5) Dr. Byrd [walked to the lectern] , [opened his book] , and [began his lecture] .

    (6) Dr. Wilson announced [that the tests were over] , [that the papers were graded] , and [that everyone had passed] .

4. Commas are used to separate two or more coordinate adjectives. Adjectives are coordinate when the conjunction *and* can be placed between them and the meaning does not change. Another method of testing whether or not two adjectives are coordinate is to reverse them. If the meaning remains the same, they are coordinate. For example, in the sentence

Martha is an ⬚intelligent⬚ , ⬚sensitive⬚ person.

the conjunction *and* could be placed between the two adjectives without changing the meaning.

Martha is an intelligent and sensitive person.

Furthermore, the two adjectives can be reversed without changing the meaning.

Martha is a ⬚sensitive⬚ , ⬚intelligent⬚ person.

On the other hand, in the sentence

Few fat men become professional basketball players.

the two adjectives cannot be reversed and written,

Fat few men become professional basketball players.

nor can the conjunction *and* be placed between the two adjectives

Few and fat men become professional basketball players.

Therefore, *few* and *fat* are not coordinate and are not separated by a comma.

5. Use a comma to separate a nominative of address, that is, the name of the person addressed, from the rest of the sentence.

   (1) ⬚Mr. Wilson⬚ , I want to recommend you for the position of chairman.

   (2) I want to recommend you, ⬚Mr. Wilson⬚ , for the position of chairman.

   (3) I want to recommend you for the position of chairman, ⬚Mr. Wilson⬚ .

6. Use a comma to separate an introductory phrase from the rest of the sentence.

   ⬚Seeking an answer to the question⬚ , the student consulted his professor.

7. Use a comma to separate nonrestrictive elements from the rest of the sentence. A nonrestrictive element is one that is not necessary for the identification of the noun to which it relates.

a. Nonrestrictive appositives

George Washington, the first president of the United States , was a native of Virginia.

b. Nonrestrictive adjective clauses

Ronald Reagan, who was born in Illinois , became the president of the United States.

c. Nonrestrictive phrases

General Dwight Eisenhower, wearing full-dress uniform , walked to the podium and began his address.

8. Use commas to separate the parts of a date.

On Monday , December 8 , 1941 , the United States declared war on Germany.

9. Use commas to separate the parts of an address.

General Brown can be located at 2168 Melody Drive , Sacramento , California , until April, when he will be transferred to Florida.

10. Use commas to set off expressions that are not necessary to the meaning of the sentence.

(1) Yes , I understand your position.

(2) By the way , where did you put my umbrella?

(3) I wonder, however , if he is as honest as he appears to be.

(4) Much to my surprise , I was elected president of the class.

11. A comma is used to show the omission of a word.

John entered a short story in the contest; Mary , a poem .

12. Commas are used to set off words of contrast.

Evening clothes, not sports clothes , are proper for the reception.

Dr. Juneau, unlike Dr. Jones , delivers interesting lectures.

13. Commas are used to set off adjectives not in their natural order.

The postman, wet and cold , shivered as he rang the doorbell.

14. A title or an abbrevation of a title that follows a name is set off by commas.

(1) E. C. Cornay, M.D. , practices medicine in my home town.

(2) Dr. Carolyn Bruder, professor of linguistics , is a graduate of Harvard University.

15. Direct quotations are separated from the rest of the sentence by a comma.

I think ," Mary said, "that the festival will be over by Friday ."

THE SEMICOLON

You will be able to eliminate errors in the use of the semicolon if you remember the four basic rules listed and illustrated here.

1. When two or more independent clauses are used in one sentence and these clauses are not connected by a conjunction, a semicolon is used to separate the clauses.

(1) Your term papers are due on May 1 ; no papers will be accepted after that date .

(2) Mr. Broussard flew to Paris for his vacation ; Mrs. Broussard motored to the Rocky Mountains .

Exception: Short, parallel independent clauses may be separated by commas.

Ex: He came, he saw, he conquered.

2. When two or more independent clauses containing commas make up a single sentence, a semicolon is used to separate the clauses.

(1) Captain Kennedy, ready for combat, marched forward ; but Lieutenant Barnes, a coward at heart, refused to move .

(2) Senator Dolan, who favored tax cuts, voted for the bill ; and Senator Friche, who was obligated to Dolan for past favors, went along with him .

3. When two independent clauses are joined by longer conjunctions such as *however, moreover, therefore,* and *nevertheless,* a semicolon is placed after the first independent clause, and a comma is placed after the conjunction.

(1) Senator Berchman is opposed to tax cuts ; however, he is in favor of reduced federal spending .

(2) John Stone's qualifications were better than those of any other applicants ; therefore, he was elected president of Saber College .

(3) Harold Jackson has an excellent batting average ; moreover, he is the best pitcher on the team .

4. Semicolons are used between a series of parallel constructions containing commas.

Jerry Jamar, a teacher ; Jacqueline Ford, a secretary ; and Ronald Treen, an engineer , were elected to the school board.

THE APOSTROPHE

The principal uses of the apostrophe are to show possession and omission. The apostrophe is also used to show plurals of letters, numbers, and words used as words.

1. The possessive of a singular noun that does not end in *s* is formed by adding an apostrophe and an *s*.

John's car
Mary's house
the sun's heat
the dog's house

2. The possessive of a singular noun ending in *s* is formed by adding either an apostrophe or an apostrophe and an *s*.

Thomas's mother or Thomas' mother
E. E. Cummings's poems or E. E. Cummings' poems
Mr. Davis's office or Mr. Davis' office

3. The possessive of a plural noun ending in *s* is formed by adding only an apostrophe.

the boys' club
the girls' dormitory
the Smiths' home

4. The possessive of a plural noun not ending in *s* is formed by adding an apostrophe and an *s*.

the women's efforts
the men's organization
the children's playground

5. The possessive of compound words is formed by adding the apostrophe and *s* to the last element of the compound.

mother-in-law's advice
someone else's books
daughter-in-law's job
sons-in-law's careers (more than one son-in-law)

6. Separate ownership is indicated by adding an apostrophe and an *s* to the name of each owner.

John's and Henry's cars (individual ownership)

7. Joint ownership is indicated by adding an apostrophe and an *s* to the last name in the joint ownership.

Emma and Elsie's store (one store jointly owned by Emma and Elsie)

8. The apostrophe is never used in writing the possessive pronouns. Always write:

yours
his
hers
its
ours
theirs
whose

9. The possessive of indefinite pronouns is formed by adding an apostrophe and an *s*.

everybody's opinion
someone's answer
one's life
everyone's answer
anyone's thoughts

10. Use an apostrophe to show the omission of a letter or letters in words and numerals.

who's (who is)
they're (they are)
o'clock (of the clock)
can't (cannot)
isn't (is not)
we're (we are)
wouldn't (would not)
Spirit of '76 (Spirit of 1776)

11. Use an apostrophe and an *s* to form the plurals of figures, letters, and words referred to as words.

The word *occasion* contains two *c*'s and one *s*.
It is difficult to distinguish between your *2*'s and *3*'s.
The +'s outnumber the −'s.
There are too many *very*'s in your essay.

THE PERIOD

The period is used in both end punctuation and in internal punctuation.

1. Use a period after a declarative sentence (a statement) and an imperative sentence (a command or request).

The roses in the garden are in full bloom.
Go to your classroom now.
Close the door, please.

Failure to use the period correctly in a series of declarative statements can result in the error called the run-on sentence. The following is a run-on sentence.

Evelyn won the gold medal, she was very happy about her success.

Correctly written, the sentence would be

Evelyn won the gold medal. She was very happy about her success.

2. Use a period at the end of an indirect question.

Dr. Bruder asked whether we had finsihed our reading assignment.

3a. The period is used to indicate abbreviations. For example,

lb.—pound
St.—Street
St.—Saint
Ave.—Avenue
Ph.D.—Doctor of Philosophy
M.D.—Doctor of Medicine
D.D.S.—Doctor of Dental Surgery
M.A.—Master of Arts
Mr.—Mister
Dec.—December
Wed.—Wednesday
N.Y.—New York

Jr.—Junior
Sr.—Senior

b. Some abbreviations are commonly written without periods. For example,

MS—manuscript
ABC—American Broadcasting Company
OED—Oxford English Dictionary

c. Abbreviations of organizations that form acronyms are written without periods. For example,

NATO—North Atlantic Treaty Organization
WAC—Women's Army Corps
SEATO—Southeast Asia Treaty Organization
UNESCO—United Nations Educational, Scientific, and Cultural Organization
CARE—Cooperative for American Relief to Everywhere

4. The period is used after an initial in names. For example,

P. R. Smith—Percival Robert Smith
John M. Lynch—John Malcolm Lynch

5. The period is used to show decimals. For example,

Money Market Certificates are presently paying 15.78 percent interest.

6. The period is used to separate dollars and cents in sums of money. For example,

$3.25
$108.15

EXERCISE 2
Mastery Test

Punctuate the following sentences correctly.

1. Mrs Robertson suggested that the *Odyssey* be taught during the first semester but Dr. Patterson vetoed the idea.
2. Before you begin writing be sure you have formulated a good topic sentence.
3. When I graded the test I found that everyones answer to the third question was correct.
4. Its time to select new textbooks.
5. Dr Jones head of the English Department announced that the scholarships had been awarded that they had been accepted and that the faculty was pleased with the selections.

6. The womens efforts to organize a volunteer group failed.
7. P R Smith was one of the leaders in organizing UNESCO.
8. We will accept his resignation when the club meets again.
9. There are certain conditions that unfortunately have to be met before you can secure the loan.
10. At the picnic we were served barbecued beef baked ham potato salad olives pickles and chocolate cake.
11. After everyone had finished the meal Dr Zimmerman suggested that we rest for thirty minutes.
12. According to his theory no one should exercise strenuously for thirty minutes after eating.
13. After everyone had rested Miss Carnes said "Its time for the baseball game."
14. Lois Harrison who was chosen captain of one team selected Mr Boyd Miss Lulac Mr Roberts Mrs Van Devanter Mrs Whiddon Dr. Greisel Mr. Weimer and Mrs Stevens for her players.
15. Mr Boyd who ran faster than any other member of the team played center field.
16. Miss Lulac on the other hand who could not run fast but who could throw a ball was the pitcher.
17. Miss Harrison told her team to observe the rules of the game to practice good sportsmanship and to make an honest effort to win the game.
18. Pleased to have been chosen as one of the team Miss Lulac picked up a bat walked to home plate and hit a home run.
19. Although they had not been on a baseball diamond in years Miss Harrisons team generally speaking played a good game.
20. However the players didnt realize how tired they were until the game was over.
21. The losing team treated the winning team to supper at Bills Restaurant.
22. Half the players ordered pizza the other half hamburgers.
23. The cook was out of hamburger patties consequently half the players had to change their orders.
24. The two teams decided to play baseball again on Flag Day which is celebrated on June 14.
25. Miss Harrison proved to be a conscientious efficient coach.
26. On Flag Day Mr Boyd wearing a baseball uniform that belonged to his son appeared at the local ball park at eight oclock.
27. Much to his surprise several of his teammates were already there.
28. The captain eager to start practicing asked everyone to take his position on the field.
29. Mr Van Devanter went to first base Mrs Whiddon went to third base and Mr Weimer strolled to the pitchers mound.

30. Mr Weimer ready for the game to begin threw the ball Mrs. Stevens the catcher did not attempt to catch it.

31. Mr Weimer the pitcher Mr Van Devanter the first baseman and Mrs Stevens the catcher delayed the game while they discussed strategy.

32. I finally took my mother-in-laws advice and applied for the position of bank teller.

33. "Were going to hire you" the bank president said "primarily because youve had some experience in banking."

34. I went to the phone dialed my mother-in-laws number and waited anxiously for her to answer.

35. "Although its too soon to know for certain" I told her "I think Im going to like my new job."

36. The bank president asked me if I wanted Tuesdays or Thursdays off.

37. On February 17 1971 I began working as a bank teller ten years later on February 2 1981 I was promoted to the position of junior vice-president.

38. My duties included approving personal loans promoting the banks services and learning the state banking laws.

39. Clarence Everett the bank president after congratulating me on my appointment asked me to meet him on Saturday May 11 at two oclock in the afternoon in Chicago Illinois for a bankers convention.

40. I drove to Chicago registered at the Belton Hotel had lunch at Susies Place and met Mr. Everett at the appointed hour.

41. Pleased to see that I was prompt Mr. Everett shook my hand and asked me if I had had a good trip.

42. I assured him that although the traffic had been heavy the trip had been pleasant.

43. "Theyre going to begin the meeting soon" Mr. Everett said "so perhaps we should find our seats."

44. During the meeting we heard some interesting speeches however the speech given by Robert Armstrong president of the First National Bank in Columbus Ohio was the most informative.

45. I agreed with everything he said about investments loans and financial security.

46. Although I had never intended to make banking my career when I was young I came away from the bankers convention convinced that I had made the right choice.

47. Its too bad that I waited until I was thirty to apply for the tellers position in the local bank.

48. Theres no way of knowing however until we try whether or not we will enjoy a particular job.

49. Of course I will always be grateful for my mother-in-laws

advice Mr Everetts encouragement and my fellow workers assistance.

50. I work hard enjoy my duties and am pleased with my success.

Parts of Speech

Nouns

A noun is the name of a person, place, animal, or thing. Nouns in the following sentences are italicized.

America has been called the melting *pot* of the *world.*
Animals in the *zoo* include *lions, elephants, tigers,* and *zebras.*
Harry, George, and *Tom* went fishing in *Mexico.*
Saudi Arabia supplies *petroleum* to the *United States.*
This *book* supplies *information* about how to survive during an *earthquake.*
The *audience* was bored by the long *speech* about the *benefits* of *Vitamin C.*

Pronouns

A pronoun is a word used in place of a noun. Pronouns include *I, you, he, she, it, we, they, me, him, her, us, them, my, mine, you, yours, his, hers, its, our, ours, their, theirs, who, whom, whose, everyone, someone, no one, anyone, that, which, each, either, nothing, another, this, these, what,* and *one.*

All pronouns have antecedents. These antecedents are the nouns for which the pronouns are substituted. An important rule to remember is that the pronoun must agree in person and number with its antecedent.

Every one of the cadets passed his test.

In this sentence the antecedent of *his* is *one,* which is singular; therefore, *his* rather than *their* must be used.

188

Verbs

A verb is a word that expresses action, being, or state of being. The verb in a sentence tells what is happening or what sets up the situation in a sentence. The verbs in the following sentences are italicized.

> Patience *is* a prerequisite for this profession.
> I *am* unsure about his motives.
> The cowboy *burst* into the room.
> James *belongs* to a fraternity.
> Most people *enjoy* a day in the country.
> Harold's father *raises* rice and sweet potatoes on his farm.
> Several of my friends *work* at the cafeteria.
> I *have* fifty dollars in my bank account.

Adjectives

An adjective is a word that describes, limits, or points out a noun or pronoun by answering the questions "What kind?" "How many?" and "Which one?"

> Colorful banners decorated the courthouse during the festival.

Colorful answers the question "What kind of banners?" and is, therefore, an adjective modifying the noun *banners*.

> Several flags fly above the building.
> *Several* answers the question "How many flags?" and is, therefore, an adjective modifying the noun *flags*.

> This dress will be worn by the bride.

This answers the question "Which dress will be worn?" and is, therefore, an adjective modifying the noun *dress*.
> The italicized words in the following sentences are adjectives.

> *Those four* cars are called *economy* cars.
> *Several* people asked *intelligent* questions about the *ultimate* results of the *new* law.
> Harry does not have *enough* money to buy himself a *new* suit.
> *Green* lawns, *colorful* flowers, and *magnificent old* trees added to the charm of Colonel Brown's *antebellum* mansion.

Adverbs

An adverb is a word that modifies a verb, an adjective, or another adverb by answering the questions "How?" "When?"

"Where?" "Why?" or "How often?" Thus they express manner (agreeably), degree (extremely), time (frequently), place (here).

Horatio sang well.

The adverb *well* tells how Horatio sang. It is, therefore, an adverb because it modifies the verb *sang*.

Marsha is an extremely good teacher.

The adverb *extremely* tells how good Marsha is as a teacher. *Extremely* is, therefore, an adverb because it modifies the adjective *good*.

A good car handles very easily.

The adverb *easily* tells how the car handles and is, therefore, an adverb modifying the verb *handles*. *Very* tells how easily the car handles and is, therefore, an adverb modifying the adverb *easily*.

The italicized words in the following sentences are adverbs.

The students were *well* prepared for college.
The policeman drove *rapidly* down the street.
Bring the paper *here* when you have *completely* finished it.
Do not submit your paper *late*.
I am *sincerely* happy about your good fortune.

Conjunctions

A conjunction is a word that joins two words, phrases, or clauses. Conjunctions can be either coordinating or subordinating. A coordinating conjunction joins words of equal rank; a subordinating conjunction introduces a construction of unequal rank.

The most common coordinating conjunctions are *and, but, or, nor, for, yet,* and *so*.

The most common subordinating conjunctions are *after, as, as if, although, while, before, because, when, whenever, where, wherever, until, that, than, unless, since, if, how,* and *though*.

Coordinate conjunctions joining words of equal rank are italicized in the following sentences.

Mary *and* Martha are sisters.
He is going *but* I am not.
We can play backgammon, checkers, *or* chess.
Jerry was well prepared, *yet* he failed the test.
Dr. Fields will not attend the meeting, *nor* will he allow me to attend.

The italicized words in the following sentences are subordinating conjunctions.

We will leave *whenever* you are ready.
I will not go *unless* you do.
He locked the barn door *after* the horse was stolen.
He will sleep *until* the sun sets.
He gets up *before* the sun rises.

Prepositions

A preposition is not easy to define but is easy to recognize because it is followed by a noun or pronoun called the object of the preposition and the modifiers of that noun or pronoun. The preposition, then, expresses the relationship of its object to some other word in the sentence. A preposition with its object and modifiers is called a prepositional phrase.

The rabbit ran across the open field.

Across is a preposition followed by its object *field* and the modifiers *the* and *open*.

The man in the blue shirt is wanted by the local police.

This sentence contains two prepositions. The first is the preposition *in* followed by the object *shirt* and the modifiers *the* and *blue*. The second preposition is the word *by* followed by its object *police* and the modifiers *the* and *local*.
Prepositional phrases can be used as adjectives and as adverbs.
The italicized words in the following sentences are prepositions.

A cross *of* gold had been placed *on* top *of* the church.
The plane flew just *above* the top *of* the building.
The driver got *into* his car and drove rapidly *down* the street.
I voted *against* the proposition.

Sentence Elements

Simple Subjects

The simple subject of the sentence is the person, place, or thing that performs the action in a sentence or tells what is spoken about in the sentence. In the following sentences, the simple subject is italicized.

Six *planes* took off at dawn.
Cardinals, blue jays, and *sparrows* can be seen in our garden.
Where did *Amy* spend the holidays?
John is an honor student.
The *student* with the best academic record will be honored at the convocation.

Predicate Verbs

The predicate verb is the word in the sentence that tells what the subject does or what the mode of being of the subject is. The predicate verbs in the following sentences are italicized.

Our teachers *are leaving* for a convention Saturday.
This book *is* a collection of poems.
The quarterback of our team *is* an honor student.
Herman *has been playing* tennis for thirteen years.

Direct Objects

The direct object is the word that receives the action indicated by the verb. The best way to locate the direct object is to ask the question "What was?" and repeat the verb. For example, to locate the direct object in the sentence

John hit his third home run.

ask yourself the question "What was hit?" The answer to that question, *home run,* is the direct object.

The direct objects in the following sentences are italicized.

James scored three *touchdowns.*
Marsha sang a *solo.*
The teacher found several *errors* in my paper.
Uncle Hiram grows *peaches, plums,* and *oranges* in his orchard.
The bride received a microwave *oven* from her parents.
Two patrolmen captured the *thief* as he ran from the store.

Indirect Objects

An indirect object names whatever receives the direct object. In the sentence

The policeman gave my father accurate directions.

the word *father* tells who received the directions and is therefore the indirect object.

In the following sentences, the indirect objects are italicized.

The pitcher threw *me* the ball.
I made my *granddaughter* a sundress.
We gave the *Salvation Army* a donation.
Mildred gave her *mother* one of her paintings.
The librarian read the *children* stories every morning.

Predicate Adjectives

A predicate adjective is an adjective that comes after the predicate verb and modifies the subject of the sentence.

These pickles are sour.

In this sentence the adjective *sour* comes after the predicate verb *are* and modifies the subject *pickle* and is, therefore, a predicate adjective.

Her dress is beautiful.

In this sentence the adjective *beautiful* follows the predicate verb *is* and modifies the subject *dress.* Therefore, *beautiful* is a predicate adjective.

In the following sentences, the predicate adjectives are italicized.

> I am *weary*.
> His motorboat is *old*.
> Our dog is *young* and *frisky*.
> My horse was *tired* after the race.
> The clouds were *dark* and *threatening*.
> The plans for the invasion were *secret*.
> The room was *clean*, but the dishes were *dirty*.
> The bells were *silent*.

Predicate Nominatives

A predicate nominative is a noun or pronoun (or any group of words such as verbals, phrases, or clauses used as nouns) that follows the predicate verb and renames the subject of the sentence. In the sentence

> Jennifer is my only sister.

the word *sister* renames the subject *Jennifer* and is therefore a predicate nominative. As a matter of fact, the two words could be reversed and the sentence could read,

> My only sister is Jennifer.

In the following sentences, the predicate nominatives are italicized.

> It is *I*.
> I am the *person* you need.
> John is a *native* of Scotland.
> The *Iliad* is an epic *poem* written by Homer.
> Alice became *president* of her sorority.
> My brother is a *member* of the faculty.
> The Broussards and the Kirks are our nearest *neighbors*.
> His ambition is *to become a doctor*.
> The problem is *what can be done with chemical waste*.

Sentences

A sentence is a group of words expressing a complete thought. Classified according to content, a sentence can be either declarative, interrogative, or imperative. A declarative sentence is one that makes a statement, such as, "Baton Rouge is the capital of Louisiana."

An interrogative sentence is one that asks a question, such as, "Which route will you take?"

An imperative sentence is one that issues a command, such as, "Go to your room."

Classified according to form, a sentence can be either simple, compound, complex, or compound-complex.

A simple sentence is one that contains only one independent clause and no dependent clauses. The following are simple sentences.

Alan Alda is my favorite comedian.
The National Geographic is a magazine of great interest to my father.
Ronald Reagan was elected president by an overwhelming majority in spite of the skepticism of the news media.

A compound sentence is one that contains two or more independent clauses but no dependent clauses. The following are compound sentences.

Harry Truman was a Democrat, but Dwight Eisenhower was a Republican.
My suitcases are packed, and my plane reservation is confirmed.
You must rewrite this paper, or you will not benefit from the corrections.

A complex sentence is one that contains only one independent clause and one or more dependent clauses. The following are complex sentences.

Although Bob ran as fast as he could, he was overtaken by Jeremiah.

She refused to identify the assailant because she was afraid that he would retaliate.

Dr. Jones will help you if you will cooperate.

A compound-complex sentence is one that contains two or more independent clauses and one or more dependent clauses. The following are compound-complex sentences.

Tommy is an honor student; but his brother Jim, who refuses to apply himself, is on the verge of failing.

Water skiing, which is a dangerous sport, is popular among my friends; but tennis, which is comparatively safe, is rarely played by these same friends.

Spring is the season when crops are planted; fall is the season when crops mature.

Clauses

A clause is a group of words containing a subject and a predicate verb. Clauses take two forms, independent clauses and dependent clauses. Independent clauses are those that make complete sense; that is, they express a complete thought. The following are independent clauses.

Babies cry.
Birds of a feather flock together.
The rabbit ran over the hill and into the cave.
Star Wars is a fascinating film.
The hurricane caused millions of dollars in damage.
A tornado is much more terrifying than a hurricane.

A dependent clause is a group of words with a subject and a predicate verb that does not express a complete thought; that is, it *depends* on the rest of the sentence for complete meaning.

where you go

is a group of words containing the subject *you* and the predicate verb *go*, but it does not express a complete thought. It is, therefore, a dependent clause. More words must be added in order for a complete sentence to evolve.

I will go where you go.

By adding *I will go* to the dependent clause, a complete thought is written.

Dependent clauses are used as nouns, adjectives, and adverbs. Dependent noun clauses can be used as the subject of a sentence, as a direct object, as a predicate noun, as an object of a preposition, or any other place that a noun can be used.

That Janie is terrified of snakes was demonstrated yesterday at the zoo.

In this sentence the dependent clause *that Janie is terrified of snakes* is used as subject of the verb *was demonstrated* and is therefore a noun clause.

Dr. Cassidy knows that my term paper will be submitted on time.

In this sentence the dependent clause *that my paper will be submitted on time* is used as direct object of the verb *knows* and is therefore a noun clause.

His excuse for being late was that his alarm clock didn't ring.

In this sentence the dependent clause *that his alarm clock didn't ring* is used as a predicate noun and is therefore a noun clause.

The professor listened to what I had to say.

In this sentence the dependent clause *what I had to say* is used as object of the preposition *to* and is therefore a noun clause.

An adjective clause is a group of words containing a subject and a predicate verb that is used to modify, that is, to describe, limit, or point out a noun or pronoun.

This is the town where I was born.

In this sentence *where I was born* is a dependent clause modifying the noun *town* and is therefore an adjective clause.

The essays that you are required to write can be either narrative or expository in nature.

Here the dependent clause *that you are required to write* is used as an adjective answering the question "Which essays?"

My grandmother could tell fascinating stories about witches who had supernatural powers.

Here the dependent clause *who had supernatural powers* is used as an adjective modifying the noun *witches*.

J. Edgar Hoover, who headed the FBI for years, has become a controversial figure.

Here the dependent clause *who headed the FBI for years* further identifies the noun *J. Edgar Hoover* and is therefore an adjective clause.

An adverbial clause is a group of words containing a subject and a predicate verb that modifies a verb, adjective, or another adverb. An adverbial clause answers the same questions an adverb answers: "How?" "When?" "Where?" "Why?" and "How often?" Adverbs thus indicate manner, time, place, reason, and frequency.

> The medical student plays tennis whenever he feels the need for a physical rather than a mental workout.

In this sentence the dependent clause *whenever he feels the need for a physical rather than a mental workout* answers the question "When does the medical student play tennis?" The dependent clause thus indicates time and is an adverbial clause.

> John rested a moment whenever the clock struck the hour.

In this sentence the dependent clause *whenever the clock struck the hour* indicates frequency and is, therefore, an adverbial clause modifying the verb *rested*.

> The troops went where their commander led them.

Here the dependent clause *where their commander led them* tells where the troops went and is, therefore, an adverbial clause modifying the verb *went*.

> In my home there is more happiness than the very rich enjoy.

In this sentence the dependent clause *than the very rich enjoy* is a dependent adverbial clause modifying the adjective *more*.

Whenever dependent clauses are written as sentences, they are called fragments and should be avoided. Dependent clauses can be used successfully as nouns, adjectives, and adverbs and can add sentence variety and thus improve style.

Verbals

Participles

A participle is a verbal used as an adjective. As the name implies, a participle is the present participle of the verb (the *ing* form of the verb) or the past participle of the verb (the *ed* form of the verb). (The past participles of irregular verbs are not formed by adding *ed* to the root form but rather are formed according to no specific rule. For example, *chosen, meant, seen, thought, drawn, driven, beaten, known, grown, given, spoken, sworn, thrown, written, fallen, brought, bought,* are past participles formed irregularly.)

Whenever the present participle or the past participle of a verb is used as an adjective, it is called a participle.

Three frightened children huddled together in the deserted house.

In this sentence there are two participles, *frightened* and *deserted*. *Frightened* is the past participle of the verb *to frighten* and is used as an adjective to describe the noun *children*. *Deserted* is the past participle of the verb *to desert* and is used as an adjective describing the noun *house*.

Falling rain impeded the rescue efforts.

In this sentence *falling* is a participle. It is the present participle of the verb *to fall* and is used as an adjective to describe the noun *rain*.

In the following sentences the participles are italicized.

A *terrified* child ran from the *burning* building.
Flying debris filled the sky.
I have an *oscillating* fan in my bedroom.

Paul was one of the *chosen* few.
The *spoken* word is often more convincing than the *written* word.

Gerunds

A gerund is a verbal; that is, it is the *ing* form of the verb used as a noun.

Jogging is good exercise.

In this sentence *jogging* is the *ing* form of the verb *to jog* and is used as a noun; in this case, as subject of the sentence. *Jogging* is, therefore, a gerund.

Fishing requires unlimited patience.

In this sentence *fishing* is the *ing* form of the verb *to fish* and is used as a noun; in this case, as subject of the sentence. *Fishing* is, therefore, a gerund.

His favorite sport is skiing.

In this sentence *skiing* is the *ing* form of the verb *to ski* and is used as a noun; in this case, as a predicate nominative. *Skiing* is, therefore, a gerund.

My mother dislikes cooking and sewing.

In this sentence both *cooking* and *sewing* are *ing* forms of verbs used as nouns; in this case, as direct objects. *Cooking* and *sewing* are, therefore, gerunds.

The gerunds in the following sentences are italicized.

My favorite sport is *swimming*.
Reading is good preparation for *writing*.
He chose *acting* as a career.
Seeing is *believing*.
Debating requires a quick mind.

Infinitives

An infinitive can be defined as the word *to* plus a verb. It is, therefore, a verbal. Unlike a gerund, which is a verbal used only as a noun, and unlike a participle, which is a verbal used only as an adjective, an infinitive is a verbal that can be used as more than one part of speech. An infinitive can be used as a noun, as an adjective, and as an adverb.

Dr. Carter wanted to succeed.

In this sentence the preposition *to* plus the verb *succeed* is an infinitive used as a noun, that is, as the direct object of the verb *wanted*.

Dr. Carter's greatest desire was to succeed.

In this sentence the infinitive *to succeed* is again used as a noun, that is, it is used as a predicate noun.

To succeed requires great effort and endurance.

Again the infinitive *to succeed* is used as a noun; in this case, as subject of the sentence.

His desire to succeed overcame all obstacles in his path.

In this sentence *to succeed* is an infinitive used as an adjective modifying the noun *desire*, that is, it answers the question "Which desire?"

He worked hard to succeed.

In this sentence *to succeed* is an infinitive used as an adverb modifying the verb *worked*, that is, it answers the questions "Why?" or "For what reason?"

In the following sentences, the infinitives are italicized.

The mayor of our town has decided *to run* for governor.
His willingness *to help* made him popular with his classmates.
The man *to see* is the personnel director.
James Taylor plays golf *to win*.
To forgive is not easy.

Verbal Phrases

Participial Phrases

A participial phrase is made up of the present or past participle of the verb and its objects, modifiers, and complements.

> American forces invading Europe during World War II liberated France.

In this sentence the *ing* verb *invading* plus the direct object *Europe* and the prepositional phrase *during World War II* is a participial phrase modifying the noun *forces.*

> Seeking a cure for cancer, scientists spend long hours in hospitals and laboratories.

In this sentence the participial phrase modifies the subject of the main clause *scientists.* The phrase is made up of the *ing* verb *seeking* plus the direct object *cure* and the prepositional phrase *for cancer.*

> The student chosen to represent our school in national competition must be charming, intelligent, and friendly.

In this sentence the participial phrase, made up of the past participle *chosen* plus the modifier *to represent our school in national competition,* is used to modify the noun *student.*

In the following sentences the participial phrases are italicized.

> Betty Galloway was the author *chosen to receive the Pulitzer Prize.*
> *Seeking a means of financing his new business venture,* Mr. Morrell called on the loan officers of all the banks in town.
> The land *occupied by the Apaches* was rich in mineral resources.
> Businessmen are wary of speculators *offering unusual returns on investments.*

Players *entering this chess tournament* must have unusual ability and stamina.

Foods *avoided by dieters* include sugars and fats.

Gerund Phrases

A gerund phrase is a gerund (an *ing* form of the verb used as a noun) plus its objects, modifiers, and complements.

Mowing the grass is not my favorite weekend activity.

In this sentence the *ing* form of the verb *to mow* plus its direct object *the grass* forms a gerund phrase used as subject of the verb *is.*

He succeeded by working furiously.

In this sentence the *ing* form of the verb *to work* plus the adverbial modifier *furiously* forms a gerund phrase used as the object of the preposition *by.*

His hobby is collecting stamps.

In this sentence *collecting stamps* is a gerund phrase made up of the *ing* form of the verb *to collect* plus the object *stamps* and is used as a predicate noun.

Discovering a cure for cancer seems to be an impossible task.

In this sentence *discovering a cure for cancer* is a gerund phrase made up of the *ing* form of the verb *to discover* plus *cure*, which is the direct object of that verb, and the modifiers of *cure.* The gerund phrase is used as subject of the sentence.

In the following sentences the gerund phrases are italicized.

Taking a short-cut through the forest turned out to be a bad idea.
Dr. Campbell enjoys *speaking to students about philosophical and mathematical concepts.*
I entertained the class by *telling ghost stories.*
His weekend tasks were *painting the garage* and *trimming the shrubs.*
I am tired of *watching television.*

Infinitive Phrases

An infinitive phrase is made up of an infinitive (*to* plus a verb) plus its modifiers, objects, and complements.

To answer a question in class terrified Joe.

In this sentence the infinitive phrase is made up of the infinitive *to answer* plus the direct object *question* plus the prepositional phrase *in class* and is used as the subject of the verb *terrified.*

He no longer wanted to build his own house.

In this sentence the infinitive phrase, made up of the infinitive *to build* plus the direct object *house* and its modifiers *his* and *own,* is used as direct object of the verb *wanted.*

His ambition to become a great criminal lawyer was realized after he successfully prosecuted the mass murderer.

In this sentence the infinitive phrase, made up of the infinitive *to become* plus the object *lawyer* and the modifiers *great* and *criminal,* is used as an adjective modifying the noun *ambition.*

In the following sentences the infinitives phrases are italicized.

To become a successful fashion model requires long hours of tedious work.
Columbus hoped *to find a western route to India.*
Gerald entered the contest *to demonstrate his skill in chess.*
To be honest is far more rewarding than *to be rich.*
The aim of the Spanish explorers was *to find gold.*

Lesson 1, Exercise 1: Basic Sentence Elements

1. The city of London, which is the capital of Great Britain and Northern Ireland, is located on the Thames River.

   or

   The city of London, which is the capital of Great Britain and Northern Ireland, is a major tourist attraction.

2. The Westminster Bridge and the buildings where Parliament meets are famous London landmarks.

   or

   The Westminster Bridge and the buildings where Parliament meets are located in London.

3. St. Paul's Cathedral is a famous landmark in London.

   or

   St. Paul's Cathedral was designed by Sir Christopher Wren.

4. The British Museum, which is famous for its manuscripts, books, and art, is visited by many tourists every day.

   or

   Many students do research in the British Museum, which is famous for its manuscripts, books, and art.

5. Since London is located on the navigable Thames River, it is a major British port.

   or

   Since London is located on the navigable Thames River, it is an important trading center.

6. When London saw its population decline during the Great Plague of 1665, new methods of fighting the plague were suggested.

   or

   When London saw its population decline during the Great Plague of 1665, many beautiful homes were left unoccupied.

7. In 1666, as a result of the worst fire in London's history, many famous landmarks were destroyed.

or

In 1666, as a result of the worst fire in London's history, many people moved out of the city.

8. When Germany bombed London during World War II, many people were killed.

or

When Germany bombed London during World War II, many buildings were destroyed.

9. London, which is Great Britain's most important manufacturing and trading center, is one of the largest cities in the world.

or

London, which is Great Britain's most important manufacturing and trading center, is also the seat of the British government.

10. Although London is a large city, it is not as crime-ridden as New York City.

or

Although London is a large city, it is still a beautiful city.

11. Because clay rather than granite lies under the surface of the city of London, it is impossible to build skyscrapers.

or

Because clay rather than granite lies under the surface of the city of London, it is easy to build subways.

12. Trafalgar Square, named for a great British naval victory, is in the heart of London.

or

Trafalgar Square was named for a great British naval victory.

13. The Haymarket, lying to the west of Trafalgar Square, is the center of London's theatre district.

or

The Haymarket, lying to the west of Trafalgar Square, attracts tourists from all over the world.

14. Plays written by playwrights from all over the world are presented in the Haymarket.

or

Plays written by playwrights from all over the world can be seen by London citizens.

15. Many bridges spanning the Thames River in the city of London are in need of repair.

or

Many bridges spanning the Thames River in the city of London were built many years ago.

16. Tower Bridge to the east and London Bridge to the west are popular and busy bridges.

or

Tower Bridge to the east and London Bridge to the west are famous London landmarks.

17. Westminster Bridge and Blackfriars Bridge are two other important and well-known bridges.

or

I visited Westminster Bridge and Blackfriars Bridge, which are two other well-known London bridges.

18. Several parks, including Hyde Park and St. James Park, are popular meeting places.

or

Several parks, including Hyde Park and St. James Park, were on my itinerary.

19. Regent's Park, containing the Zoological Gardens, is another famous London park.

or

Regent's Park, containing the famous Zoological Gardens, is popular with the children of London.

20. The University of London, founded in 1836, attracts students from all over the world.

or

The University of London was founded in 1836.

Lesson 2,
Exercise 1:
Compound Subjects

Group 1
Both Australia and New Zealand are island countries located in the South Pacific.

Group 2
North Island, South Island, and Steward Island are the three large islands that comprise the country of New Zealand.

Group 3
Wellington, the capital of New Zealand, and Auckland, its chief port, two of New Zealand's largest cities, are located on North Island.

Group 4
Dairy farming and sheep raising are the two chief sources of farm income in New Zealand.

Group 5
English and Maori are the two languages spoken in New Zealand.

Group 6
Sydney, the capital of New South Wales; Melbourne, the capital of Victoria; and Brisbane, the capital of Queensland, are the three largest cities in Australia.

Group 7
William Dampier and James Cook were the first two Englishmen to visit Australia.

Group 8
Willem Jansz and Abel Tasman, both Dutchmen, were the first Europeans to explore the continent of Australia.

Group 9
The duckbilled platypus, the emu, and the lungfish are three unusual animals that can be found in Australia.

Group 10
The wombat, the kangaroo, and the koala are three Australian marsupials, that is, animals that when young are carried in an outside pouch on their mothers.

Group 11
The eucalyptus tree, which is native to Australia, and the wattle or acacia, which grows in the dry inland regions, are two of the most frequently seen trees on the continent.

Group 12
Sugar cane and pineapples are the two leading crops grown in the wet, warm, tropical coastal plains of northeastern Australia.

Group 13
Cool summers; abundant rainfall, which provides ample grass; and large cities, which provide markets for dairy products, combine to make dairy farming the principal agricultural industry along the southeastern coastal plains of Australia.

Group 14
Sheep raising and wheat farming are the two principal occupations west of the Eastern Highlands, which divide the coastal plains from the rest of Australia.

Group 15
Wheat and wool are the two principal Australian exports.

Group 16
Dingoes, or wild Australian dogs that kill sheep; rabbits, which eat vast quantities of grass in sheep country; and droughts, which stunt the growth of grass, are three major problems faced by Australian sheep ranchers.

Group 17
Manufacturing, mining, and trading contribute to the Australian economy.

Group 18
The British Commonwealth of Nations, Japan, and the United States provide the principal markets for Australian exports.

Group 19
Lead, gold, silver, and zinc are the principal metals mined in Australia.

Group 20
Uranium in the north and oil in the west are two recent Australian discoveries.

Lesson 3, Exercise 1: Compound Predicate Verbs

1. The cowboy mounted his dapple-gray horse, picked up the reins, and went off in search of the stray cow.

2. Dr. Hirt walked to the lectern, opened his notebook, and began his lecture on Greek drama.

3. Mrs. Dobie started her car, backed down the driveway, and hit a tree.

4. The comedian walked to the edge of the stage, looked at the audience, and began telling outrageously funny stories.

5. Indians in Santa Fe, New Mexico, make jewelry and sell it to tourists visiting their city.

6. Benjamin Franklin, one of America's great statesmen, invented bifocal glasses, discovered that lightning is a huge spark of electricity, and started the magazine that became the *Saturday Evening Post.*

7. Galagos, or "bush babies," which are strange little animals found in Africa, hunt for their food at night, curl up in trees during the daytime, and sleep until dusk.

8. The Federal Bureau of Investigation solves crimes committed against the United States, investigates the backgrounds of government workers, and guards against enemy spies during wartime.

9. James Madison helped write the Constitution of the United States, served as Secretary of State under Thomas Jefferson, and became the fourth president of the United States.

10. Spanish farmers cultivate grapes to be distilled into wine, grow olives to be processed into oil, and raise tobacco to be made into cigarettes and cigars.

11. The sandpiper lives on the seashore, digs in the sand for insects, and follows receding waves searching for shellfish.

12. Daniel Boone, a famous American pioneer, fought against the Indians, helped settle the state of Kentucky, and finally moved his family to Missouri.

13. Douglas MacArthur, a graduate of the United States Military Academy at West Point, fought with the Allied forces in France during World War I, was supreme commander of the Allied forces in the Southern Pacific during World War II, and served as overall commander of the United Nations forces during the Korean conflict.

14. Herbert Hoover served as head of the American Relief Administration in Europe after World War I, was Secretary of Commerce under President Harding and President Coolidge, and became the thirty-first president of the United States.

15. Susan B. Anthony, a pioneer in the fight for women's rights, advocated the abolition of slavery; founded the first state temperance society; and was largely responsible for the passage of the 19th Amendment to the U.S. Constitution, which gave women the right to vote.

16. Chester Nimitz served in the submarine fleet during World War I, was Allied commander of the Pacific Fleet during World War II, and later became a cabinet advisor to the Secretary of the Navy.

17. William Penn, a pioneer American, founded the state of Pennsylvania, planned the city of Philadelphia, and helped in uniting the American colonies in their revolt against England.

18. William Howard Taft was named Secretary of War in Theodore Roosevelt's cabinet, was elected the twenty-seventh president of the United States in 1908, and was appointed Chief Justice of the United States Supreme Court in 1921.

19. Voltaire, one of the most important French writers and thinkers, composed satiric verse; wrote a short novel, *Candide*; and attacked both the church and the state in his *Philosophic Dictionary*.

20. Robert Edwin Peary, a famous Arctic explorer, discovered the North Pole in 1909; proved that it was the center of a large, ice-covered sea; and claimed that Greenland was an island.

Lesson 4, Exercise 1: Compound Direct Objects

1. For many years before the Europeans came to America, Indians had been growing corn, potatoes, squash, and beans.

2. American Indians built huge burial mounds, stone-faced pyramids, and limestone temples.

3. The first Europeans believed that all Indians were uncivilized, that they all looked alike, and that they were scalp hunters.

4. The Indians tried to follow their tribal customs and to obey their tribal laws.

5. The terraced adobe houses of the Pueblo Indians contained large rooms for food storage, underground rooms for religious ceremonies, and apartment-like dwellings for hundreds of families.

6. Not a warlike people, the Pueblos wanted to live in peace, to tend their farms, and to weave colorful cotton and wool cloth.

7. The Apache Indians, a warlike tribe, fought and defeated the Spanish explorers, the United States army troops, and the American settlers.

8. The Europeans introduced smallpox, measles, tuberculosis, and influenza, diseases that wiped out thousands of American Indians.

9. The typical Indian woman of the central plains wore deerskin moccasins and leggings as well as one-piece dresses decorated with colorful beads.

10. Indian warriors hunted deer, buffalo, bear, and moose for food.

11. For traveling up and down streams, the Indians built canoes of birch and elm bark and boats of animal hide stretched over a wooden frame.

12. American Indians occupied grass houses, birch-bark tepees, and earth-covered hogans.

13. Indians in the South occupied raised dwellings roofed with palmetto leaves and cabins built of logs.

14. To transport goods Indians used sleds drawn by dogs; baskets strapped to their own backs; and the travois, made of long poles covered with skins and pulled by horses.

15. Indians introduced succotash, a dish made of beans and corn; baked beans; and steamed clams to the Pilgrims.

16. Indians wore headpieces made of porcupine quills and animal hair, war bonnets fashioned of eagle feathers, and turbans made of brightly colored cloth.

17. Indian warriors in the Northwest wore wooden body armor and helmets.

18. Instead of metal, Indians used wood, bones, and stone to make their tools.

19. In their purification rites, Indians included a potion that caused violent vomiting, hot baths that resulted in intense sweating, and shampoos that expelled evil spirits.

20. For recreation Indians played lacrosse and chenco.

Lesson 5, Exercise 1: Compound Predicate Nominatives

1. Three pioneers in the science of space travel were Konstantin E. Tsiolkovsky, a Russian; Robert H. Goddard, an American; and Herman J. Oberth, a Hungarian-born German.

2. The three types of manned spacecraft developed by the United States are the Mercury, which carries one man; the Gemini, which carries two astronauts; and the Apollo, which accommodates three men.

3. The three types of manned spacecraft developed by the Russians are the one-man Vostok, the three-man Voskhod, and the four-man Soyuz.

4. The three types of space probes that travel to other parts of the solar system are the unmanned lunar spacecraft, designed to study the moon; the planetary probes, designed to collect and transmit information about planets such as Venus and Mars; and interplanetary probes, designed to orbit the sun.

5. The first three United States astronauts were Alan B. Shepard, Jr., who rode the spacecraft Freedom 7; Virgil I. Grissom, who made a suborbital flight; and John H. Glenn, Jr., who rode Friendship 7, the first U.S. spacecraft to orbit the earth.

6. The first two Russian cosmonauts were Yuri A. Gagarin, who orbited the earth in Vostok 1, and Gherman S. Titov, who orbited the earth seventeen times in one flight.

7. The three men involved in the first moon landing were Neil Armstrong, Michael Collins, and Edwin Aldrin.

8. The three parts of the Apollo spacecraft were the service module, which held the fuel tanks; the command module, which housed the astronauts on their journey to and from the moon; and the lunar module, which actually landed on the moon.

9. The three major problems facing space scientists are overcoming earth's gravity, staying in orbit, and getting back to earth.

10. The only two countries in the world to put man into orbit around the earth are Russia and the United States.

11. The three largest lakes in South America are Lake Maracaibo, Lake Patos, and Lake Titicaca.

12. Precious stones mined in South America are Colombian emeralds and Brazilian diamonds.

13. The three largest South American cities, all of which have a population of over three million, are Sao Paulo and Rio de Janeiro, both in Brazil, and Buenos Aires in Argentina.

14. Two South American heroes are Simon Bolivar and José de San Martin, leaders in the fight for independence from European domination.

15. Three of the chief exports and sources of wealth in South America are Venezuelan petroleum, Argentine cattle, and Peruvian copper.

16. The two official languages of South America are Portuguese, spoken in Brazil, and Spanish, spoken in the other nine countries.

17. Most people living in South America are Europeans and their descendants; native Indians; and mestizos, a mixture of Europeans and Indians.

18. The three main objectives of present-day South American officials are to build industries, to eradicate communicable diseases, and to improve education.

19. The two earliest explorers in South America were Christopher Columbus and Francisco Pizarro, both in the service of Spain.

20. Two highly civilized Indian tribes that the first Europeans found in the New World were the Incas of Peru and the Aztecs of Mexico.

Lesson 6, Exercise 1: Compound Adjectival Modifiers

1. Scotland's breathtaking scenery includes the barren, rugged, windswept mountain peaks of the Western Highlands.

2. Loch Lomond is the most beautiful, the largest, and the most celebrated of Scotland's numerous lakes.

3. Scotland's heritage is reflected in many ancient, well-preserved, and spectacularly beautiful castles.

4. Tiny, peaceful, and picturesque villages dot Scotland's landscapes.

5. The Wicklow Mountain area of Ireland is a remote, solitary, and awesome region of enormous forests and winding streams.

6. Connemara is one of the most colorful, isolated, and romantic regions of Ireland.

7. England's Stonehenge is a unique and mysterious prehistoric collection of stone pillars thought to be the remnants of ancient temples built by sun worshippers.

8. The Dublin Horse Show, an annual international event, takes place in early August.

9. One of England's favorite tourist excursions is a motor trip through the lush, sparsely settled countryside to Windsor Castle.

10. Many tourists think of France as an interesting, beautiful, and colorful country.

11. Paris, the capital of France, is a large, charming, and beautiful city.

12. The French are an independent, hard-working, and thrifty people.

13. Notre Dame Cathedral, located in Paris, is a magnificent and world-renowned example of medieval Gothic architecture.

14. The social centers of Paris for natives and tourists alike are the popular and picturesque sidewalk cafés.

15. Many Bretons, occupying the northwestern part of France, are frugal, industrious, seafaring people.

16. Many chateaux, or mansions that dot the French countryside, were moat-surrounded, relatively impregnable feudal citadels of French landlords.

17. Today these chateaux are well-preserved, government-maintained tourist attractions.

18. One of the architectural phenomena of France is the famous medieval island monastery, the Abbey of Mont St. Michel.

19. The French Riviera on the Mediterranean coast is a popular, internationally known gathering place for the world's jet set.

20. In southeastern France the tourist meets the swarthy, fiercely independent, and unusually courageous Basques of the Pyrenees Mountains.

Lesson 7, Exercise 1: Compound Adverbial Modifiers

1. The guide reluctantly yet graciously led the tourists into the underground cavern.

2. One of the tourists loudly and emphatically announced that he would go no farther.

3. The frightened tourist had heard that the floor of the cave was gradually and mysteriously disappearing.

4. Everyone in the group quickly and forcefully demanded that the tour be canceled.

5. The guide immediately and eagerly suggested that the tourists explore the ancient ruins above ground.

6. The guide told us that the Aztec Indians conquered the native tribes of central Mexico easily and completely.

7. After the conquest the Aztecs slowly and patiently created a magnificent empire.

8. In 1519 the Aztecs, in turn, were ruthlessly and completely conquered by Hernando Cortez, a Spaniard who came to the New World in search of gold.

9. Soon Cortez virtually enslaved the Aztecs.

10. For four hundred years the people of Mexico stoically yet resentfully endured domination by greedy and unscrupulous administrators.

11. During these four centuries a few concerned leaders attempted courageously but unsuccessfully to establish a democratic form of government.

12. Finally, in 1924, and fortunately for the Mexican peasants, Plutarco Elías Calles was elected president.

13. Calles relentlessly and systematically expropriated large tracts of land owned by a few wealthy Mexican families and foreign investors.

14. These large tracts of land were divided equally, whether communally or individually, among more than two million Mexican families.

15. Proud of their new ownership, the Mexican peasants worked long and diligently to make their farms successful.

16. In the last fifty years, as a result of land reform, the standard of living in Mexico has risen dramatically and continuously.

17. In spite of such rapid reform, about half of Mexico's population still lives dangerously near or below poverty level.

18. Thousands of Mexicans ultimately migrate illegally to the United States.

19. The United States Immigration Service has conscientiously but unsuccessfully attempted to halt such illegal entry.

20. Both the Mexican and the American governments have worked untiringly but fruitlessly to institute new emigration and immigration policies.

Lesson 8, Exercise 1: Combining Sentences by Using Participial Phrases

1. Switzerland, often called the playground of Europe, attracts tourists from all over the world.

2. The Swiss people, motivated by a strong desire for freedom, have a truly democratic form of government.

3. The three official languages spoken by the Swiss people are German, French, and Italian.

4. The Rhaeto-Romantic language, spoken in only one canton, is similar to Latin.

5. The president of Switzerland, elected by the Federal Assembly for one year, cannot immediately succeed himself.

6. Railroads tunneling through the mountains of Switzerland make year-round travel possible.

7. The Mittelland Plateau, lying between the Jura Mountains on the north and the Alps on the south, is one of the principal land routes of central Europe.

8. In Bern, Switzerland, tourists can wander leisurely up and down quaint winding streets lined with picturesque little houses built of green and yellow limestone.

9. In Lucerne the tourist is encouraged to explore the medieval Mill Bridge decorated with grim scenes of the Dance of Death.

10. The city of Brienz, known worldwide for its beautiful and unique wood carvings, attracts many tourists to Switzerland every year.

11. Lake Lucerne, surrounded by beautiful forests and snowcapped mountains, offers some of the most breathtaking scenery in Switzerland.

12. Quaint little villages huddled against the spectacular Swiss mountains provide quiet, peaceful inns for the exhausted tourist.

13. San Moritz is often referred to as the Queen of the Alps because of its many resort homes occupied by royalty and millionaires.

14. Chillon Castle, immortalized by the English poet Byron in "The Prisoner of Chillon," is located at the edge of Lake Geneva.

15. "The Prisoner of Chillon," based on the life of François de Bonnivard, is largely fictional rather than factual.

16. Framed by the distant Alps, the cobalt blue waters of the Lake of the Four Forest Canons offer a scene of unsurpassed beauty.

17. A trip to Switzerland would be incomplete without a visit to Montreux, located on the shores of Lake Geneva.

18. In Lucerne the tourist can enjoy a spectacular view of the Alps by taking the cable car extending to the top of Mount Rigi.

19. Tourists, impressed by the warmth and hospitality of the Swiss people, often plan to make a return trip to this fabulously beautiful country.

20. Switzerland, nestling between France and Germany, has been strangely free from war for more than a century.

Lesson 9, Exercise 1: Compound Gerunds and Gerund Phrases

1. Salmon and trout fishing as well as skiing and mountain climbing lure visitors to Argentina's Lake District.

2. Visitors to Buenos Aires enjoy strolling along Avenida 9 de Julio, the widest boulevard in the world, and visiting Plaza de Mayo, the city's heart and the birthplace of Argentina's independence.

3. Drinking tea at a *confeteria* on Calle Florida and eating charcoal broiled steaks at *La Cabaña* are two gustatory delights for the tourist in Buenos Aires.

4. The tourist should not leave South America without visiting the jungle area on the Argentina–Brazil border and exploring the two-and-a-half-mile-wide Iguassa Falls.

5. Two exciting side trips for the visitor to Rio de Janeiro include taking the cable car to the top of Sugarloaf Mountain and driving through Tijuca Rain Forest to Carcovado Peak.

6. The tourist interested in early South American civilization should spend a day examining the Incan baths at Tambomachay and exploring the Incan fortress at Sacsahuaman.

7. A morning in Lima can be divided between shopping for gold and silver, ceramics, and woolens and visiting the cathedral on Plaza de Armas, where the remains of Pizarro lie.

8. After flying from Lima to Iquitos and traveling by motorboat twenty miles down the Amazon River, a person can visit the Amazon Safari Camp.

9. The tourist can also fly east from Lima to the Island of Baltra for the purpose of boarding a yacht and cruising the Galapagos Islands.

10. A cruise of the Galapagos Islands offers a variety of experiences, such as talking with the scientists at the Charles Darwin Research Station and observing the sea lion nurseries on South Plaza Island.

11. A visit to James Island in the Galapagos offers such opportunities as seeing the remains of an old salt mine or photographing a colony of fur seals.

12. In Ecuador the tourist should insist on visiting Quito, the national capital, and seeing the Equatorial Monument as well as La Compania Cathedral.

13. A motor trip from Quito south to Latacunga offers the tourist the opportunity of driving through the Valley of Volcanoes and observing many unusual rock formations.

14. Tourists in Bogota, the capital of Colombia, enjoy visiting the famous Gold Museum and ascending Monserrate Mountain in a cable car.

15. Tourists in Cartagena, Colombia, can choose between watching a good soccer game and relaxing on the sun-bathed beaches.

16. Other tourist attractions in Bogota include shopping for Colombia's famous emeralds and visiting the beautiful underground Salt Cathedral.

17. Its many rivers and coastal waters make Uruguay famous for its fishing and boating.

18. The visitors to Montevideo, the capital of Uruguay, can enjoy visiting the many beautiful rose gardens in the daytime and seeing an excellent theatrical production in the evening.

19. Two new experiences for the Uruguayan tourist are drinking *Yerba maté,* a Latin American tea, and eating *asado con cuero,* a steer cooked in its hide.

20. Understanding the needs of Third World nations and appreciating the contributions of Latin American artists are two possible results of a visit to South America.

Lesson 10, Exercise 1: Compound Infinitive Phrases

1. The O'Toole family planned to go to Ireland to visit their ancestral home and to become acquainted with relatives whom they had never seen.

2. After much discussion, the O'Tooles decided to fly to Dublin and to stay at a small family hotel in the center of the city.

3. This type of lodging would enable the O'Tooles to meet and to talk with Irish natives rather than with other American tourists.

4. A central location in Dublin would make it possible for them to walk to many places of interest and to save money in transportation fees.

5. On the evening of their arrival, the O'Tooles arranged to have dinner in their rooms and to retire early.

6. Before retiring, however, Mr. O'Toole called the hotel manager to compliment the food and to ask to be awakened at six o'clock the following morning.

7. The next day the four O'Tooles decided to go their separate ways and to meet at the hotel for dinner at six in the evening.

8. Mr. O'Toole intended to visit the Census Bureau and to examine the O'Toole family records.

9. Mrs. O'Toole wanted to shop in the stores along O'Connell Street and to buy souvenirs for her friends at home.

10. Katie O'Toole planned to telephone an old college friend and to invite her to lunch.

11. Peter O'Toole decided to visit the University of Dublin and to examine the records concerning the Easter Rebellion.

12. Peter's research would enable him to collect the missing data he needed and to complete his article for the *Journal of Irish History*.

13. Mr. O'Toole wanted to find the address of his second cousin, Michael O'Toole, and to discover the names of other O'Toole relatives.

14. Mr. O'Toole's lifelong desire to find his cousin and to learn the names of other living relatives led to a family reunion within the week.

15. After the reunion the O'Toole family left Dublin to visit their ancestral home in Cork County and to go to the Castle of Blarney, where they kissed the Blarney Stone.

16. According to legend, a person who kisses the Blarney Stone acquires the power to speak eloquently and to persuade his listeners to do as he would have them do.

17. After leaving Cork County, the O'Tooles toured the countryside to see the ruins of ancient ivy-covered monasteries and to enjoy the Lakes of Killarney and other magnificent Irish scenery.

18. Finally the O'Tooles visited the west coast of Ireland to hike along the coastal cliffs and to enjoy the wide expanse of lonely beaches.

19. At the last minute the O'Tooles decided to return to Dublin and to fly back to the United States from there.

20. For many years the O'Toole family would be able to remember with pleasure their visit to Ireland and to know that family ties to the old country were not yet broken.

Lesson 11, Exercise 1: Combining Sentences by Using Adjective Clauses

1. Our European trip took us to the Iberian Peninsula, which includes the countries of Spain and Portugal.

2. In Portugal we visited the capital city of Lisbon, which is located on the right bank of the Tagus River.

3. An interesting Spanish city on our tour was serene and colorful Seville, which lies in the center of Spain's wine country.

4. In Granada we saw the Alhambra, a centuries-old Moorish castle, which is a melange of marble courts, patios, mosaics, and gardens.

5. Farther north in Toledo we toured El Greco's museumlike home, in which some of the great works of this famous Spanish artist are displayed.

6. The Prado Museum, which houses the largest collection of El Greco's paintings, is located in Madrid.

7. The enormous monastery palace of Escorial, which was built by Philip II, contains priceless tapestries, works of art, and crypts of Spanish kings.

8. The Valley of the Fallen, which lies near Madrid, is a moving memorial to those who died in the Spanish Civil War.

9. Northwest of Madrid the tourist can visit Palencia, which is the site of Spain's oldest university.

10. Santiago de Compostela, which is an ancient Spanish town located in northwestern Spain, was a center for pilgrimages for hundreds of years.

11. A beautiful eleventh-century cathedral, which is said to be the spiritual resting place of St. James the Apostle, is also located in Santiago de Compostela.

12. From Spain we went to Italy, which is a boot-shaped peninsula jutting into the Mediterranean Sea.

13. Rome, which is an ancient yet modern city located on the Tiber River, was our first stop in Italy.

14. In Rome, which is probably the most historically significant city in Europe, one can visit, among other landmarks, the Vatican, the Pantheon, the Appian Way, and the Sistine Chapel.

15. The Vatican stands on the *Vaticanus Mons,* or Vatican Hill, which got its name because it was the meeting place of the ancient *vaticinatories,* or soothsayers.

16. The Pantheon, which was built by Agrippa, son-in-law of Augustus, who was the Roman emperor from 27 B.C. to 17 A.D., has been used as a Christian church since the seventh century.

17. The Appian Way, which goes from Rome to Brindisi by way of Capua and which was begun in the fourth century B.C., is the oldest and best of all the Roman roads.

18. The ceiling of the Sistine Chapel, which was built in 1473, is decorated with the famous frescoes painted by Michelangelo.

19. North of Rome on the Arno River lies the beautiful city of Florence, which has often been called the storehouse of the world's art treasures.

20. Still farther north in spectacular Venice one can visit the famous Bridge of Sighs, which connects the palace of the doge with the state prisons and over which prisoners were once escorted from the courtroom to the scaffold.

Lesson 12, Exercise 1: Combining Sentences by Using Adverbial Clauses

1. After we bought our tickets and checked our bags at Kennedy International Airport in New York City, we boarded a Pan American jet liner bound for South America.

2. Although we could have toured the major cities such as Rio de Janeiro and Buenos Aires, we decided instead to see such out-of-the-way places as Iguassu Falls and the Galapagos Islands.

3. Because torrential rains greeted us at Lake Titicaca, we were unable to enjoy the hydrofoil boat ride across the lake.

4. Not until we arrived in Montevideo at noon did we discover that a gaucho barbecue had been arranged for us at Faraut's Winery.

5. Yields on many small South American farms are poor because the farmers are unacquainted with modern farm equipment and methods.

6. Because the piranha, a flesh-eating fish, is found in many South American rivers, swimming in these rivers is a dangerous pastime.

7. After the South American section of the Pan American Highway was completed in the 1960s, it was possible to travel from Ecuador to Argentina by car.

8. An automobile trip across South America is not always comfortable because some sections of the highway are rough and dusty in dry weather and muddy and treacherous in wet weather.

9. Because such exotic birds as egrets, toucans, flamingos, and parrots are found in large numbers in South America, ornithologists, or those who study birds, like to visit there.

10. If a tourist wants a look at lush tropical plantations; breathtaking mountain scenery; swirling river currents; and quiet, secluded

lakes, he should spend two days traveling on a local train from Guayaquil to Quito, a distance of about three hundred miles.

11. Because Venezuela is blessed with many miles of excellent highways, the best way to see the country is by car.

12. Because superhighways have made the adjoining coastal area easily accessible to Caracas, many people who work in the city live in beautiful homes and apartments along the coast.

13. Because it is located in a valley about 3,000 feet above sea level, Caracas enjoys mild temperatures throughout the year.

14. The Venezuelan *llanos,* or plains, which lie between the mountains and the Orinoco River, are a hunter's paradise because many wild animals and exotic birds live there.

15. After we left Venezuela in early May, we flew to Paraguay, a small country lying between Brazil and Argentina.

16. Although visitors to small Paraguyaan villages are impressed by the clean adobe houses and the neat village square, they are unaware that these towns have no modern conveniences such as electricity, running water, and sewage systems.

17. After we spent a week seeing as much of the Paraguayan countryside as possible, we left for Uruguay.

18. Although Uruguay is the smallest republic in South America, its people enjoy the highest standard of living as a result of vast reforms, which broke up large plantations and gave the land to the people.

19. As we drove for several hours through the streets of Montevideo, the capital of Uruguay, we were impressed with the many parks filled with beautiful trees and colorful flowers.

20. Although we did not have time to visit the Island of the Lions, which is famous for its seals and sea lions, we did have a good view of the island as we left Montevideo by plane for home.

Lesson 13, Exercise 1: Paragraph Construction: The Basic Elements

1. Students attend college for reasons that vary from the frivolous to the serious.

2. During the past year terrorism and violence have increased dramatically throughout the world.

3. A large number of foreign students with a variety of interests makes up the student body at the University of Southwestern Louisiana.

4. The fifty-five-mile-an-hour speed limit on the nation's highways has had beneficial results.

5. Louisiana is truly a sportsman's paradise.

6. The Bank of Commerce and Trust Company offers its customers several savings plans with interest rates ranging from 5 to 17 percent.

Index

V